The Leo Burnett Book of Advertising

Edited by Simon Broadbent

Business Books

London   Melbourne   Sydney   Auckland   Johannesburg

Business Books Ltd
An imprint of Century Hutchinson Ltd
Brookmount House, 62–65 Chandos Place, London WC2N 4NW

Hutchinson Publishing Group (Australia) Pty Ltd
PO Box 496, 16–22 Church Street, Hawthorn, Melbourne, Victoria 3122

Hutchinson Group (NZ) Ltd
32–34 View Road, PO Box 40–086, Glenfield, Auckland 10

Hutchinson Group (SA) (Pty) Ltd
PO Box 337, Bergvlei 2012, South Africa

First published 1984
Reprinted 1986
© Leo Burnett Ltd 1984

Set in 10 on 13 point Meridien by the Pen & Ink Book Co. Ltd
Printed and bound in Great Britain by
Anchor Brendon Ltd, Tiptree, Essex

British Library Cataloguing in Publication Data
The Leo Burnett book of advertising
 I. Advertising agencies – Great Britain –
Case studies
 I. Broadbent, Simon
 659.1'125'0941   NF6182.G7

ISBN 0 09 155980 4

Contents

Introduction

Making advertising which actually sells the products advertised is usually hard work. To do the job properly means methodical thinking and as much checking as is feasible — as well as creative talent. If we are also to understand after it appears just what advertising has achieved, then there is more work to be done — which we hope results in better advertising next time.

Work in an advertising agency starts outside the agency — with a manufacturer who sees a chance to sell more, and more profitably, with advertising. It is *his* opportunities which motivate our work, though this book concentrates on the advertising agency's role.

The advertising agency with major accounts is a complicated place where a number of different skills are required. The goals of this book are to describe the major techniques used and to give examples of their application. The specialists write about their skills; in the second part we see these skills linked in case histories describing effective campaigns.

The major steps taken when making advertising determine the subjects of the chapters on technique.

First an advertising strategy is agreed; this is part of a larger marketing plan and will stimulate and guide those who write the advertisements. Next we must respond to the brief with advertising which is fresh and convincing to the target consumer; we know this as 'creative' work since it is impossible to reduce to a formula, but some generalizations and guides to success can be suggested, some experience can be passed on. It is often our objective to build a brand, based on a long-running campaign.

Meanwhile a media plan is written to carry this message in an economical and effective way. The advertising idea is executed on film, tape or paper. After the campaign, we evaluate our work in the field.

In real life, of course, the process is not so neat: there are steps backward and there are shortcuts. There is quality control, blood, sweat and tears.

It is these main steps we describe here — those directly involved in planning, making and placing advertisements — though they are not the only ones. Some of the backbone of an agency is omitted. The front-line troops are supported by people producing and handling data and printed information, by buyers and accountants; they are co-ordinated by client service, intimately involved in orchestrating the specialist contributions, making the whole team move as one, bringing the client into our decisions and us into his. The reason this particular job is not described separately is that it emerges in the case histories (largely written by client service people).

All of those who wrote for this book work at Leo Burnett, London. Advertising ideas and advertisements themselves come from individuals, but the whole of an advertising campaign is a team product. This book has only one purpose — to show how we make sales-effective advertising — but many hands have been employed.

An advertising agency has to have inspiration and principles. We need a point of view on how to make great advertising, though we do not have a formula.

Leo Burnett in London is a second-generation agency. Leo opened his shop in Chicago in 1935; he died in 1971 at the age of 79. The traditions he laid down are respected today. But we have to learn from the record, from affectionate remembrance by Leo's collegues or from what he himself wrote. To communicate what it is like to work for a great creative leader, the book starts with a short biography. It is a recollection of our Chicago headquarters in the 1960s. The quotations should enthuse advertising people anywhere, but particularly in this agency.

We are grateful to all our advertisers, and particularly to those who have allowed us to publish case histories. Leo Burnett said: 'I have learned that you can't have good advertising without a good client and that you can't keep a good client without good advertising.'

In 1983—4 we worked for the following clients:

Apple Computers (UK) Ltd	Bayer UK Ltd
Aqualac Springwaters Ltd	Beecham Foods
Austin Rover Group Ltd	Beecham Proprietaries
Bacardi (Europe) Ltd	Booker McConnell Plc

Bovril Ltd
Bradford & Bingley Building Society
British Bakeries Ltd
H P Bulmer Ltd
Cadbury Ltd
Cathay Pacific Airways Ltd
Central Office of Information
Chambourcy Food Company Ltd
Chivers Hartley
Domecq UK
Express Newspapers Plc
Fisher Sales UK
General Accident Fire & Life Assurance Corporation Plc
Green Giant Company Ltd
Kellogg Company of Great Britain Ltd
Kimberly-Clark Ltd
Memorex UK Ltd
Milk Marketing Board
National Benzole Company Ltd
National Westminster Bank Plc
The Nestlé Company Ltd
Nicholas Laboratories Ltd
Nikon (UK) Ltd
Philip Morris Ltd
Procter & Gamble Ltd
Sanyo Marubeni (UK) Ltd
Schott Glass UK Ltd
Scottish & Newcastle Breweries Ltd
Seven-Up Great Britain Incorporated
Unipart Ltd
United Airlines
Wild Fowl Trust
WonderWorld Theme Park
Yorkshire General Life Assurance Company Plc

The chapters on Flake, Super Noodles, Lucozade and Metro are based on papers published in *Advertising Works* (1980 and 1982), from the Advertising Effectiveness Awards, with the permission of the Institute of Practitioners in Advertising.

The chapter on Simplicity is based on the paper which won the 1982 Lord Rothermere Radio Award.

The chapter on Leo Burnett is based on reminiscences by Carl Hixon, and the permission of *Advertising Age* is acknowledged. The American illustrations are reproduced with the permission of Philip Morris Inc., the Kellogg Company and Leo Burnett Company Inc.

The cover design is by Mike Brant.

The authors are listed below. It has been a pleasure to work with them all.

Dennis Barham   Chairman
Gareth Bogaerde   Head of TV Production
Fiona Campbell   Head of Radio Buying

Alan Cooper	Senior Planner
Chris Dickens	Media Director
Jackie Dickens	Head of Planning
Jeff Fergus	Deputy Managing Director
Mo Fisher	Planning Director
Mick Foley	Head of TV Services
Lionel Godfrey	European Coordination Director
Steve Greensted	Account Director
Rick Holmes	Board Director
Jocelyn Horsfall	Deputy Head of Planning
Brian Jacobs	Associate Media Director
Delores Lane	Media Supervisor
Paul Lazell	Board Director
Vic Margiotta	Board Director
Gerry Miller	Creative Director
Ailean Mills	Account Supervisor
Mia Ospovat	Planning Director
Bob Peach	Board Director
Lynne Sacks	Senior Account Manager
Bob Stanners	Creative Director
Pamela Vick	Account Director

Explanation of the glossary

No technician can explain what he does without using technical terms. But many readers of this book will be puzzled by some words like 'doublehead', 'TVR' or 'regression'.

A reader who knows something about one or more of our special subjects will be irritated if we have to say every time 'the stage in producing a TV commercial when the sound is on one piece of film, the picture on another', or 'percentage of target who are exposed to a commercial', or 'a technique which examines how one measurement varies with one or more others'. Nor will such people want to read the whole of a glossary of technical terms.

Our solution is to give a glossary at the end of the book, as well as an index. The first time we use a word which is in the glossary, it is printed in bold type in the text. Words in the index which are also in the glossary are in bold too.

You can then look up the word if you want, or go on reading if its meaning is already clear to you.

1

Who was Leo?

Leo Burnett, for all of his fame and influence in the American advertising world, was a shy man, not given to public appearances. The best place for Leo-watchers to observe him was at meetings of the Creative Review Committee, where he spent most of his time.

This was the creative centre-court at Burnett. It was manned by the agency's senior people and its function was to approve the advertising before it went to the client. In doing so, it subjected the work to every form of examination imaginable by a wolf pack of professional scrutineers.

Leo's appearance was singularly in contrast to the popular notion of a great advertising chieftain. He was short and slope-shouldered, with a paunch. His waistcoat and lapels were sprinkled with ash from the Marlboros he smoked. A large double chin gave him a faintly froggy aspect at times, and when he spoke, his voice was a gruff burble. The front of his head was bald and freckled.

Leo's most memorable feature, however, was his prominent lower lip; of which more later, as it figured importantly in all our lives.

No photograph of Leo ever captured his true aspect — ill-assorted, perhaps, but glowing with a Pickwickian radiance of good humoured dignity, plus something else, difficult to fathom at first, which later revealed itself to be his formidable force or will.

On good days, when the work was approved, Leo clapped his hands softly and beamed: 'Goddamn good!' — his highest-ever accolade.

On bad days, however, when the work was not approved, the meeting was apt to devolve into a fine mess. Within minutes after an exhibit went up on the wall, there appeared an unmistakable clue to its fate. It was Leo's lip, and as the presentation progressed all eyes were riveted upon it. If Leo liked what he was seeing, his lip remained *status quo*. If not, it began to cantilever forward disapprovingly while the wretched presenter – who could see this close-up – struggled on, and the creative group's uneasiness turned to dismay.

Often at this point Leo would spin round in his chair, lower his head and begin to scribble what we all knew was to be a bill of particulars against the work; or sometimes he wrote *finis* to the proceedings then and there, a process he referred to as 'instant democracy', by blurting out in the midst of the presentation: 'Look,' like Churchill announcing that the 2nd Panzer Division had broken through at Dunkirk, 'we're in real trouble! Call the client and cancel the meeting. We've got lots of work to do.'

This pronouncement would be followed by groans, eyeball rolling and elaborate paper crumpling by the creative group, while the account people looked on sympathetically.

These were character-revealing moments. There would sit Leo like a stone wall off which the creative group's best shot had just ricocheted. Deep in each man's gut was a sinking feeling, because (1) he was not sure he could top what had just taken him weeks to create, (2) he was whacked, but knew he would be working all night again, and (3) his wife would be mad as hell.

Different people reacted in different ways. On one occasion John Matthews, the agency's copy director, methodically and accurately lobbed one dozen small Kellogg packages the length of the room, over Leo's head and into the wastebin as Leo was reading out his indictment of them. He didn't once look up.

Rudy Perz, creator of the Pillsbury Doughboy, having seen one of his recommendations demolished by a broadside from Leo, strode to the door, turned to the CRC and with martyred dignity announced: 'Lions 3, Christians nothing,' before stalking out.

The cigar, however, must go to Andy Armstrong, one of the agency's early creative directors and the original model for the Marlboro cowboy. During a particularly stormy review at which Leo rejected Andy's creative entry and fielded one of his own, Andy rose quietly from the table, left the room, hailed a taxi to the station, bought a ticket on the Super Chief and entrained for California. In California he sat for a few days in the sun, thought about life, caught the train back to Chicago, re-entered the room, resumed his seat and rejoined the battle. Observers say that Leo never blinked, going or coming. His response on these occasions was always to withdraw into his dignity and ride out the squall.

Later he wrote: 'Have the courage to go back to the client with a better idea whenever you can find one, even if he has already OK'd the ad and is well satisfied with it.'

He also understood that advertising made by the agency has to be sold: 'I have learned that no client will ever buy better advertising than he understands, or has an appetite for.'

And that we and the advertiser have to live together: 'I have learned that a good ad which is not run never produces sales.'

All of the *sturm und drang* in the Creative Review Committee, however abrasive it sounds in the telling, was in fact meat and drink to the creative troops. The process had a wholesome, yeasty effect on the making of advertising — and of advertising people. Leo enjoyed every minute and once wrote: 'Looking back over our greatest creative achievements I recall that few of them were generated in an atmosphere of sweetness, light and enthusiasm, but rather one of dynamic tension, complicated by off-stage muttering.'

The creative ranks loved Leo and were proud of him. He rode at the head of their dusty column and the white plume of his principles could always be seen in the thick of battle, bobbing above the *mêlée*.

They were principles of attitude, rather than dogma. In place of rules, he had constructed a creative ethic, made up of such emotional convictions as 'Clichés are unacceptable', 'Good advertising lifts up, not tears down', 'Nothing is ever good enough around here', 'We want people to say "What a great product", not "What a great ad"', 'Keep it simple', 'Know the rules but be willing to break them', and 'Too many ads that try not to go over the reader's head end up beneath his notice.'

But never: 'Show the package in the first ten seconds' or 'Name the product in the headline.'

Leo's central convictions were as follows.

The most powerful advertising ideas are non-verbal, and take the form of statements with visual qualities made by archetypes. Their true meanings lie too deep for words: a strong man on horseback, a benevolent giant, a playful tiger. The richest source of these archetypes is to be found at the roots

New from Philip Morris

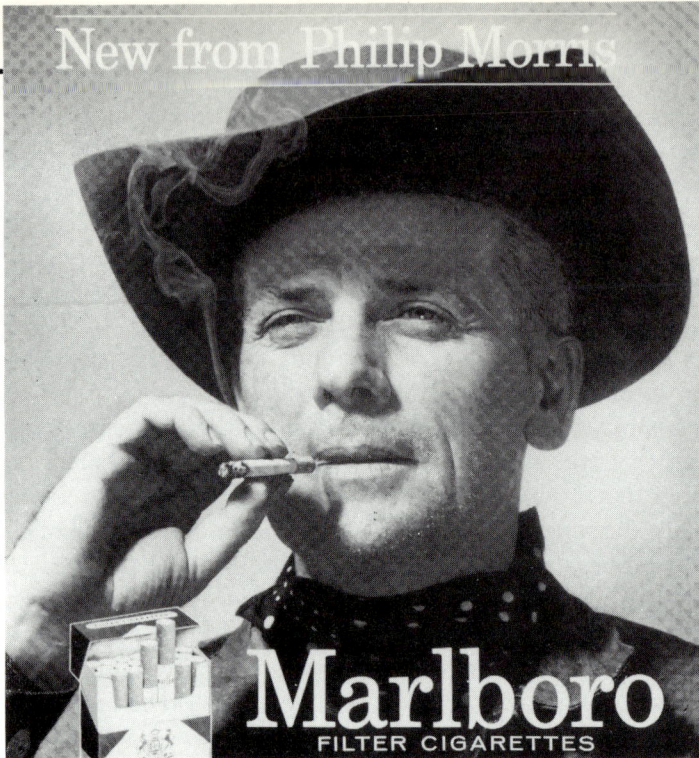

Marlboro
FILTER CIGARETTES

NEW FLIP-TOP BOX
Firm to keep cigarettes from crushing. No tobacco in your pocket

Marlboro
LONG SIZE

POPULAR FILTER PRICE

The new easy-drawing filter cigarette that delivers the goods on flavor. Long size. Popular filter price. Light up a Marlboro and be glad you've changed to a filter.

(MADE IN RICHMOND, VIRGINIA, FROM A NEW PHILIP MORRIS RECIPE)

The Marlboro Cowboy:
USA

of our culture — in history, mythology and folklore.

Somewhere in every product are the seeds of a drama which best expresses that product's value to the consumer. Finding and staging this *inherent drama of the product* is the creative person's most important task: 'Do not lean on tricks, devices or "techniques". Keep the advertising *relevant* — shun irrelevant approaches in headlines and illustrations, no matter how clever they are.'

One of the greatest dangers of advertising is that of *boring* people to death. An advertising audience deserves to be rewarded for its time and attention.

The secret of all effective originality in advertising is not the creation of new and tricky words and pictures, but of putting words and pictures into new relationships. Leo was fond of quoting an old boss of his on this subject, who had advised him: 'If you insist on being different just for the sake of being different, you can always come down in the morning with a sock in your mouth.'

The Jolly Green Giant we know today — still selling corn

Frosties' Tony the Tiger

Leo had many such sticking points, and one of his most adamant was *believability* — not only accuracy, but the believability that accrues to something which is appropriate. He had a built-in detector that whooped and clanged at the first whiff of codswallop. If an advertisement or commercial failed to observe the fitness of things — if it didn't 'thump' right like a good watermelon — Leo's detector sounded off. 'I don't believe it!', he would mutter, shooting out his lip and turning his back on the offending work.

Akin to this was Leo's confidence in what he called the creative person's 'wee, small voice'. He described it as 'your best source of inspiration for ideas, your best copy research, your best test market ...'. 'The saddest sight of all,' he wrote, 'is the good creative person who loses confidence in his own judgement and intuition — who tunes out that little voice and listens only to the voices of other people.'

Another of his convictions was the belief that 'God is in the details'. By this he meant that the creative task only begins with the identification of the idea. What happens next, in the painful, cameo-carving process of giving this idea shape, texture and colour, is what determines greatness in advertising.

What he demanded was perfection. What he got on most days fell short of that, but was way ahead of anything his perspiring followers hitherto had considered their best efforts.

Working for the Burnett agency in this environment was a

heightened experience — a forcing house for talent and professionalism. Some thrived on it. In other cases it was enough, as Leo wrote, 'to send strong men staggering away to buy a goat farm'. But even at the worst of times one felt bound to the agency with hoops of steel. The strongest of these, stronger even than the sweet talk of headhunters on the make, was one's relationship with Leo, and the feeling of clansmanship.

It was rather like being a kid again, in a big rambunctious household over which Leo presided as *paterfamilias*, dispensing approval, punishment, instruction, advice and sticking plasters.

It tickled Leo to acknowledge his paternity. 'Well, boys and girls, ...' he would say; and the fact that the 'boys and girls' he was addressing might include one white-haired vice president, a towering ex-marine colonel and a grandmother struck neither him nor us as out of order.

Leo put his faith in people, not in things. He was fond of repeating that 'our whole inventory goes up and down on the elevators every day'. Together with most of his founding attitudes, this one has been retained deep in the grain of the agency.

Leo's true love was reserved for those people who shared not only his standards and desire, but his mystical vision of advertising as a great, positive force — bigger, even, than the marketplace which it serves. To be included as a member of this group by Leo could become, as C S Lewis said of pain, 'an intolerable compliment'. But in return for what he expected and extracted, he nurtured them, put opportunities their way and did his best to smooth their paths. It was a symbiotic relationship: neither party could progress without the other.

★

Leo was born in a small Michigan town in 1892. His father, as Leo told it, intended to name him George, but an accident of penmanship and abbreviation caused the birth certificate to read not 'Geo' but 'Leo', where the matter came to rest.

His father was a local merchant, and Leo's earliest recollection of advertising was seeing the store name and slogan on the umbrella which shaded the delivery cart. Years later, in his corner office on the fifteenth floor of Chicago's new Prudential Building, he would write: 'I'm not city-bred. In the Michigan town where I was raised you could hear the corn growing on hot nights. I snuck up on Chicago, slowly, by way of outlying cities. When I finally got there I was forty years old and confirmed in my colloquial ways.'

Perhaps in his shyness he learned to 'imaginate' himself out of himself and into the identities of other people, where he could feel their feelings and understand their wants. Most good creative people share this odd, wistful experience of being extra-social, detached from their own society and therefore able to travel easily in their imagination to another, where − like watchers from a distant planet − they observe and relate but never belong.

Leo, in his sixties, had the vitality of a Cape Buffalo, and no one could stay with him for more than a few laps. David Ogilvy had cannily noted this phenomenon, and remarked recently that he had once rejected a merger proposal from Leo for one principal reason: 'Leo was the only man I knew who worked harder than I do,' he recalled. 'The thought of Leo's ringing me in New York at 2 a.m. and asking me to meet him in Chicago for breakfast with some fresh campaign ideas was more than I could bear.'

So intense was his absorption that when working on a hot project it was necessary to lock up copy and layouts each night before leaving. Otherwise the shadowy figure of Leo would materialize later that evening for a sneak preview of the goodies.

In his seventies a low blood sugar condition caused him to grow faint at times, and on one occasion gave rise to the most spectacular of testimonials to his stubborn client loyalty. A number of client and agency people were sitting at a poolside in Key Biscayne, Florida, where Kellogg held their annual marketing meeting. Leo was holding forth. Suddenly his voice grew weak, he dropped and collapsed onto the table.

'Candy bar', he whispered.

One of the group had already leapt to his feet and was hurdling chairs on his way to the vending machine when Leo lifted his head and cried hoarsely: 'Make sure it's a Nestlé!'

★

Leo Burnett's effect on advertising, and on the industry he loved, continues to be incalculable.

He invested advertising with new social values by demonstrating that it is a force which not only sits at the right hand of business, but is a powerful means of expressing national identity and pride: which can serve the country's economy, then go on to plow something of great value back into the social ecology.

In the process, he created a mythology for our time in the pages of national magazines and on hundreds of millions of television screens, in the form of advertising which 'draws up a lot of nourishment from the richness of American folklore, restores it, and perpetuates it in a keen and lively sense', as he described it.

In 1967 he said to his assembled staff: 'Let me tell you when I might demand that you take my name off the door:

'When you forget that the sheer fun of ad-making and the lift you get out of it − the creative climate of the place − should be as important as money to the very special breed of writers and artists and business professionals who compose this company of ours − and make it tick.'

'When you lose your passion for thoroughness ... your hatred of loose ends.'

'When you stop reaching for the manner, the overtones, the marriage of words and pictures that produces the fresh, the memorable and the believable effect.'

'When you disapprove of something, and start tearing the hell out of the man who did it, rather than the work itself.'

'Finally, when you lose your respect for the lonely man − the man at his typewriter or his drawing board or behind the camera or working all night on a media plan. When you forget that the lonely man − and thank God for him − has made the agency we now have possible.'

Part I
Techniques

2
Effective advertising strategies

By working to a strategy, we ensure we get advertising which is relevant as well as impactful. Strategy should be settled before creative work begins. Creative people contribute to the strategy, but that is additional to writing an advertisement to the strategy.

Writing a good creative strategy is arguably the most difficult task in the whole process of developing advertising. It requires a combination of careful, deductive thinking and imaginative flair. The writer needs not only to be able to see the wood for the trees, but then to think how the wood *might* become if the trees were changed. The task is, in its own way, every bit as creative as designing an advertisement.

The strategy is essentially a statement of what the advertising is trying to do. It is both the base on which advertising is developed and the action standard against which creative work will be judged. It is also part of the media brief.

One of the hallmarks of a good strategy is that it cannot be misinterpreted. There is an internal communication problem if the strategy is loosely written. A woolly strategy results in creative people focusing on their own interpretations of what it means. The resulting creative ideas may be judged inappropriate, because they fail to meet the way others interpret the strategy. Misdirected creative effort results not only in wasted work, but consequent lowering of motivation and morale.

A strategy will sometimes be rewritten when creative teams have started to look for a creative solution. It could be argued that an advertising strategy does not really exist until it has been executed. If a strategy does not lead to distinctive, relevant advertising, it may be the strategy which needs to be reconsidered, rather than the ability of the creative people to execute it. This is particularly important where the advertiser's own planning procedures contain statements of strategy following corporate guidelines. These are difficult to alter once the formal plans have been approved.

At Leo Burnett we have our own way of writing a strategy, setting out the five key points it should contain. These discipline our thinking, although we may modify the way we write strategies according to the advertising problem. When the advertiser has his own internal disciplines we usually write the strategy in a form which is acceptable to him but check that nothing is omitted which we feel important.

The five parts of the written strategy, which we detail later, are the advertising objectives, target, consumer proposition, justification and tone.

Before these are written, there is work to be done. We start by getting to grips with the market, the brand's position in it and the relation of the consumer to the brand.

We review what we currently know about the product or service we are to advertise. If we do not know enough, we ask for more. If more cannot be afforded, we make judgements.

At this stage, **client service** and planner work closely with the manufacturer. Client service seeks to understand the nature of the advertising problem within the broader marketing perspective. The planner attempts to define the advertising task from the standpoint of consumers' perceptions of the market. Both disciplines work alongside each other, and their roles overlap.

The market

The descriptions which follow, of the information we look for about the market, veer towards idealism. In practice it is not common for us to have access to detailed knowledge of *all* the factors outlined. Small manufacturers may not have extensive consumer research data; in newly developing markets (see the Super Noodles example) we may, of necessity, have to learn as we go.

The nature of the familiarization task also depends on whether we are dealing with a product or service which is new to us, or with a long-standing account. In the former case, we shall be starting from scratch; in the latter, we may have to try to wipe the slate clean and re-think.

The biggest difficulty in a review of the current status of a product or service is that of conducting a detailed analysis of all the relevant factors whilst maintaining a holistic approach to the advertising problem. Like studying biology at O-level, one learns the skeleton and, separately, the digestive system. But one ends up with little clue as to where the hard bits are in relation to the soft bits, or why things should be so arranged. The proper task is less one of 'swot' and more one of 'sift'; it is not a question of knowing everything, but finding out what matters. We have to end with something simple, with a motivating idea, not with a market description. It is this choice of one fact, one attitude, one association, which leads to memorable and effective work.

We start with a physical product, such as a certain liquid in a bottle or powder in a box − or a service, such as a contract with a building society or insurance company. Part of our job is to turn this into a brand. A brand has a personality. The buyer and the user should relate to it more as they do to a person than to a thing. A brand is worth more than a product. A product may change dramatically − a new bottle or box, a new formulation, a different rate of interest. A brand remains the same, or changes only slowly.

We have to understand both the product or service in the forms an engineer or accountant might use *and* the brand which its users know.

In particular, what is the *current status* of the brand? *Why* is the brand in that position? In which *direction* should the brand be moved in order to fulfil the marketing and financial objectives? What *role* can advertising play in helping to move the brand in the desired direction?

The nature of the market within which the brand operates, and how this market is defined. It is worth bearing in mind that many 'markets' or market segments are manufacturer-defined, based on differences in manufacturing processes (for example moulded bars *v* countlines in the confectionery market, fortified wines *v* white spirits in the alcoholic drinks market). Such distinctions may be irrelevant to the consumer (who keeps dry vermouth and vodka in totally separate mental boxes when considering what to drink?). We need to understand how consumers perceive the market context − which other products or brands they believe are in competition with our brand and why.

The history of the development of the market. We want to understand which factors have affected this development. We look at:

- The *current size* of the market, in terms of value and volume.

- The *direction* of the market (growth *v* decline) in terms of real value and volume.

- *The factors which have affected the development* of the market. These may be many and various. For example, changing cultural trends, such as the effect of healthier eating on some food product categories; price over time, relative to the retail price index and to broadly competitive product categories; technical innovations − for example, home video and computers. Sometimes factors which have affected the development of a market may be fundamental and irrevocable − for example, the effects of changing population structures or the size of the potential market for products aimed at children. Sometimes they may be the basis of a consumer proposition, the annexation of territory in the consumer's mind for our brand, although general in themselves.

Segments existing within the market, how they are defined, and how meaningful they are to consumers. In some markets, **segmentation** originally developed as a result of **product innovation** (for example, granule *v* powdered instant coffee); some were based on understanding and exploiting differing consumer needs (for example, shampoos for dry *v* oily hair); some developed in response to changes in related product categories (for example, washing powders for automatic machines). In order to understand the options open to us for the brand or service we are advertising, we need to know within which segment(s) of the market it is currently positioned, why, and whether there may be opportunities for change or modification.

Understanding the nature of consumer purchasing patterns within the market. Many of the opportunities here are for marketing exploitation rather than for advertising. It is not easy to distinguish between the two. Questions we ask ourselves are:

- What is the **penetration** of the product category and how has this changed over time?

- What is the typical **buying cycle** − the interval between purchases − and why? A frequent, almost automatic, choice once a week or more often (bread), or a rare, considered decision (cars, building societies, banks).

- To what extent is the market **seasonal**, and why? − for example, the massive seasonality of boxed chocolates, resulting from gift purchases for Christmas, Mother's Day and Easter.

- Does the market show any **regional bias**, and what are the reasons for this? For example, in some food and drink markets, regional sales differences are based on historical manufacturing, distribution or consumption patterns.

Understanding the trade structure, and nature of distribution for the market as a whole. How dependent are volume sales on different types of retail outlet? To what extent might there be opportunities for exploiting outlet categories (for example, developing confectionery sales through garages)?

Determining the historical levels of marketing support for the product category over time, and the balances between above- and below-the-line expenditure. To what extent have brands within the market been heavily price promoted? How fierce is the competition for an advertising share of voice?
    Some markets are notoriously difficult to get to grips with. The beer market is an example. This is very complex in its regional differences, based on the historical importance of local breweries, and their associated distribution channels. The on-licence trade structure is completely different from the off-licence structure, and each has many sub-divisions. Different types of product and packaging are sold in different outlets (for example, draught beer *v* cans). There are seasonal elements in the market, especially in relation to lager. The market has been changing considerably over the years, with the increasingly competitive situation in the lager market, and the growth of real ales and regional brands. It is clearly necessary to understand how such a market operates before one can start to develop an advertising strategy for a brand within it.

The position and performance of the brand or service within the market

Having understood the dynamics of the market within which we are competing, we must next determine where this brand or service currently stands and why it is in this position. Throughout our analysis of the brand's position, we will be comparing its performance with that of the market overall, and with specific competitors.

We start by looking at **ex-factory sales** or the equivalent, together with industry data, continuous audit data and/or consumer panel data to understand the brand's volume sales and share over time. We will be looking specifically to see whether our brand differs from competitors', for example in terms of sales volume by region or seasonal sales patterns.

Having done this, most of the subsequent questions we shall be asking relate to *why* the brand or service is in this position. We shall be examining the following factors.

Distribution. Does our brand's pattern of distribution compare favourably with competition and, if not, why not? Do opportunities exist for increasing distribution through traditional outlets or gaining new distribution through new outlets?

Pricing strategy. Where does the brand fit into the pricing structure of the market? What is the justification for any marked difference between the price of our brand and those of competitors? Have pricing policies been consistent over time? To what extent is our brand price sensitive; that is, how do sales shares react to price?

Whilst always important, this is particularly critical when we are selling services or durables, for which consumer experience does not occur until after the buying decision has been made!

The reader will recognize two aspects of all these questions. First, they are wider than usually thought necessary for writing an advertising strategy. This is because we are at this stage also acting as marketing consultants for our client, helping him to clarify his marketing , and even his manufacturing, plan. And we need to explore every avenue, in case round some corner we come across an advertising idea. Second, we shall repeat this list when we come to discuss the evaluation of our campaign, our attempt to disentangle what advertising achieved from the effects of other factors. The analysis required to understand the market (is distribution the key?... is our brand **price-sensitive**?) is very similar to the analysis of how sales changes were achieved, treated in a later chapter.

Product. Finally, we shall be looking at the product itself in some detail. With a new product, or one which is new to us, we seek to discover its technical strengths and weaknesses. For a new car, we need to understand in detail how it measures up to competition in terms of specification, performance, fuel economy, etc. For a food product, does it have any specific recipe or ingredient advantages? We then look at consumer product testing, both blind and branded if available, to ascertain consumer perceptions of the product's relative strengths and weaknesses. Here we look, not just at attitudes towards the basic product, but also price, packaging, and any other relevant aspects of the total mix. We are particularly concerned to determine the extent of perceived product strength or image strength or, usually, some combination of the two.

It may be stating the obvious, but everyone in the team will try the brand themselves, use it in different ways, get to know it well. This is particularly important for the creative people. It is also why sympathy with the product, if not a prerequisite, is an advantage in everyone on the team.

The consumer relationship with the brand

Having determined how the brand or service we are dealing with performs in the market, we look in detail at consumer behaviour and attitudes:

■ *We need to identify who buys the brand,* from analyses of panel data or usership and attitude studies. We also need to consider who uses and consumes the brand, and who influences purchase decisions.

For example, where products are bought for child consumption (cereals, snack foods, confectionery), children may influence the choice of brand. Pets can have an influence in choice of petfood.

■ *We have to understand the nature of the buying decision —*

whether it is considered, impulsive or routine; whether it is a low or high risk.

We also need to determine how frequently the brand is bought, and why different consumer sub-groups (for example, heavy, medium, light users) buy the way they do.

■ *We need to look at how the brand is used,* and whether it is used in different ways by different people. For example, some confectionery products are more likely to be solus eats, while others are shared. Some (like Flake and Bournville Dark) can have culinary uses. Microcomputers are bought by different people for radically different uses. Cider can be a pub pint or a family meal accompaniment drink.

Crucially, we must understand consumer motivations for purchasing and using the brand concerned. Are motivations different from those which apply to the category as a whole? To what degree are motivations conscious and rational, or unconscious and irrational? In some product fields (for example, toothpaste, washing powders, many durables and services) consumers may be primarily seeking functional benefits. In others (for example, chocolate bars, bath additives) sensual benefits may be primarily motivations for brand choice. In some (for example, alcoholic drinks, perfume, newspapers) the image benefits which accrue from display and use of the brand may be key motivators.

Whilst quantitative usership and attitude studies provide much of the hard data relating to patterns of buying and using products, it is to qualitative research that we often look to gain an understanding of the motivations to buy a given brand. By providing in-depth information about a range of individual cases, qualitative research can often better help us to group the different users and ways in which they relate to the brands they buy.

Getting the strategic solution

Reaching the best strategy is never easy — there is invariably more than one reasonable solution. When we have analysed all the relevant information, and determined the current status of the brand, there is often considerable debate amongst members of the **core group** working on the account to determine what to do.

Further research may be undertaken at this stage to explore a range of positions, or to help choose the most motivating way of conveying a particular product advantage or consumer benefit. Such research is usually qualitative; it often entails using a range of stimuli to get consumer reactions to the options open to us. **Concept boards**, each describing a different product proposition (or describing the same broad proposition in different ways) may be used. When we are seeking to define the ideal image for a brand, a series of pictures of different people, of home interiors, leisure pursuits, or holiday locations (probably cut from magazines) prove useful stimuli for helping to evoke the current image of a brand, and the ideal self-image of its user.

Once creative teams have started to try to execute the strategy, their rough executions, and the research which may be set up to examine their worth, help us to refine the strategy further. As discussed earlier in this chapter, it can be argued that a strategy does not exist until it has been executed. Sometimes a creative team will light upon an interpretation which provides insight as to how the strategy itself could be tightened – particularly useful for subsequent executions in a campaign.

No one expects strategy development to be an easy, or an exact, task. Deductive thinking is essential, but intuition and imagination are important too. Let us turn again to the key defining criteria, to examine precisely what should be recorded in the strategy.

Advertising objectives

Defining the objectives for advertising is the most important element in strategy development, as the objectives will govern the other decisions.

When defining the advertising objectives, we are setting out to answer two broad questions:

■ Where do we want our brand or services to get to in the marketplace?

■ What role should advertising play in helping it to get there?

In order to reach the desired goal, the manufacturer uses a whole range of marketing and sales resources, of which advertising is only one. Hence it is essential for us to take a clear and realistic point of view as to what part advertising can play in helping to achieve the goals set.

The objectives of advertising should define *whose* behaviour we are seeking to influence, and in what *direction* — for example, persuading existing users of a food product to serve it more frequently to their families, or encouraging non-users of a brand to try it. The statement of objectives should then go on to describe how we expect advertising to achieve the desired effect on behaviour; for example, by providing the target with new information about a brand, suggesting how it can meet specific needs, and so on.

Advertising may have either direct or indirect roles; in some cases we may need different advertising to play different roles for the same brand.

For example, on the most direct level, advertising can seek to sell 'off the page' (for example, mail order) or to provoke a direct and immediate sales response (for example, to announce a specific promotion or sale). Other, more direct objectives of advertising may be to stimulate trial of a brand, by announcing its arrival on the market, or communicating a product change or improvement. Specific, tactical advertising may seek to prom- ote seasonal sales of, say, boxed chocolates for Mother's Day gifts, or alcoholic drinks for Christmas consumption.

In a more indirect way, advertising may seek to modify or reinforce attitudes to a brand, relating it to key consumer needs or reminding consumers of particular benefits, functional or emotional. Indeed, for many of the big brands we handle (for example, Cadbury's Flake, Bulmers Strongbow) the strategy of reinforcing positive brand attitudes and values has remained similar over many years.

It is critical to ensure that advertising objectives are realistic; that is, that they are achievable and affordable. Advertising cannot easily raise a brand's sales within a declining market, or radically change the image of an established brand with one burst of a new campaign.

Target audience

We should be clear whether we are targeting advertising

primarily towards current buyers or users of our brand (heavy or light, frequent or occasional) or non-users. Given appropriate data, it is a relatively simple matter to ascertain who our target is in terms of demographic classifications (i.e. sex, age, marital status, presence of children, etc). Women buy many products which are consumed by other family members, and in some cases husbands or children have an important influence on the brand bought.

There may also be secondary targets for advertising, which we may have to bear in mind — for example, the client company's workforce, salesforce or the trade. Whilst specific advertising or publicity may be directed towards these groups, there may also be a requirement to ensure that the main consumer campaign is supportive of, or at least does not alienate, one or more of these sub-groups.

When defining the target for advertising, we cannot rely on demographic classification factors alone. We need to understand what our targets are like, in terms of life style, their general attitudes towards the product category and motives for purchase. For example, with a food product, we need to understand the eating patterns of our target audience; how they relate to meal preparation; what is most important in this context (for example, healthier diet, varied diet, home cooked food). Depending on the product, it may also be useful to describe our target in terms of their enjoyment or otherwise of cooking, the extent to which they experiment with foreign foods, and so on.

We may have life style research that can help us to understand and define our target audience. Leo Burnett have conducted several life style studies, in the USA and the UK and other countries. The most recent UK study (1981) concentrated on relating a wide range of statements covering consumer attitudes, opinions, and interests to buying behaviour across a broad range of product fields, and use of media. This has enabled us to compare, for example, the attitudes and life styles of users of a product category compared with non-users, or buyers of one brand compared with buyers of another.

Consumer proposition

The consumer proposition should constitute a single-minded

statement of the communication objectives of the advertising; the most important thought we want the target audience to take out of the advertising. For the creative team, this will be the crux of the strategy, and the more single-minded the proposition, the greater is the opportunity for an innovative, creative solution to be reached.

When reviewing all the information and research we have about our brand or service, we compare it with those of competitors, in order to find a positioning which is competetive, original, and motivating to consumers. First we consider whether we believe the basis of our proposition derives from a genuine product advantage, some way in which our brand is better than the competition. We must be sure that any product advantage is important in motivating purchase in order to translate it into a strong selling proposition. When we launched the Austin Metro, the 83 miles per gallon at 30 miles per hour we were able to claim constituted a strong product advantage over competitive hatchbacks, and was successfully used as a key proposition in the launch campaign.

However, with many of the brands we advertise, there will not be genuine product advantages which distinguish the brand from competition. We then look to see whether the brand or service has a *perceived* advantage over competition, possibly image-based, which we can build to present a motivating proposition to the consumer. For example, deriving from its name and the heritage of consumer advertising (using the device of the famous arrows) Bulmers Strongbow cider is perceived to be a brand with more male appeal than that of many competitors, a fact which has been built on in different ways over the years when positioning the brand.

Where we cannot readily present a specific product or image-led advantage for our brand, we look at the opportunities for a **generic positioning**, which can be executed in a unique and branded way. This means identifying the key motivation for purchase in the product category, and conveying this as a benefit which our brand can provide. The long-standing and highly successful Cadbury's Milk Tray campaign has consistently done just this. The 'Man in Black' campaign rewards both givers and receivers of boxed chocolates by conveying the trouble the giver has taken to choose a box of chocolates he knows the receiver will really enjoy ('All because the lady loves Milk Tray').

In many cases the proposition will take a specific product advantage, and relate it to a broader consumer benefit to produce branded and motivating advertising. With the main Flake campaign, the 'crumbliest, flakiest milk chocolate in the world' claim is the more motivating because the escapist, indulgent benefits which derive from eating the bar are dramatized.

Justification

The justification should set out the evidence to support the consumer proposition. In some cases it will be desirable for the justification, or 'reason why' we are making a particular claim for a brand, to be spelt out in the advertising. In many instances, however, this will not be considered necessary or desirable.

Where the consumer proposition seeks to convey a specific product advantage through advertising, the justification will generally contain the product evidence to support this (for example, known performance ratings for a car, tooth decay prevention ingredients for a toothpaste). Where the proposition is based on conveying perceived advantages for a brand (or correcting perceived weaknesses in image) research-based evidence of consumer attitudes and beliefs may be used. If the proposition is basically generic, evidence as to why we believe a generic claim will be motivating will be detailed, again often based on research evidence.

Tone

This section of the strategy provides guidelines to the tonal qualities we believe the advertising should have. Very often these tonal qualities will be required to reflect the brand's personality, or to project the personality we desire for the brand. For example, we may require advertising with a contemporary tone if we are seeking to rejuvenate a brand's image; an authoritative tone of voice may be more effective if we are seeking to convey technical innovation in a durable product field.

The tonal values of advertising are especially important when we are communicating with a tightly defined target group (for example, young male pub drinkers). If they are to respond to the advertising, it must be of their genre. They must feel empathetic towards the medium as well as the message. In such instances, phrases denoting desired tonal qualities are inadequate. It will be critical for the creative team really to understand their target − their life style, needs and aspirations − in order to communicate with them effectively.

Examples of strategies

What should emerge is a clear and simple conclusion. Much of the work done to reach this conclusion never sees the light of day. We have to lead the users of the strategy through description to prescription. Having made our choice, we have to set it up and defend it. The defence is inevitably a summary of what we know about the market, the brand and its consumers.

Consider the examples described in the case histories later in the book. Summarizing them, we can write one- or two-sentence strategies:

Flake: Position Flake as enjoyed by a wider variety of people than its heaviest users, and tackle head-on the messiness of eating it.

Super Noodles (Year 1): Make housewives with children, especially instant mashed potato users, try Super Noodles as an alternative to potatoes.

Body Mist: Retain Body Mist's position as a woman's deodorant but present it as the most powerful solution against sweat.

Lucozade: Position Lucozade as a replacement for lost energy in health, rather than as an aid to recovery in convalescence.

Sunday Express: Show existing readers that they should stay loyal − or they would miss the enjoyable features of the Sunday Express and its Magazine.

Simplicity: Surprise sanitary towel users into a re-evaluation of the brand as the safest full-size press-on towel.

Perrier: Flatter the mineral-water buyer that he or she is buying a stylish, distinctive and exclusive brand in choosing Perrier.

Metro: Position the car as a hatchback offering economical family motoring. Persuade people who want to buy a British car that this is a superior product.

The actual strategies were, of course, very much fuller. They ensured that everyone involved understood the relevant facts about the past as well as what was intended for the brand's future.

The creative brief

The creative brief is obviously based on the strategy, but is more than this alone.

It is a very specific piece of communication, written for creative people, rather than for the advertiser, and when writing the brief we must have creative needs most in mind.

A good brief should work on a number of levels. It tells creative people what the advertising task is that we are asking them to fulfil. It also gives creative people understanding and insight into the brand and the advertising target. Hence it needs to be descriptive, evocative and interesting to read.

Thirdly the brief, and the verbal briefing which invariably accompanies the written brief, can help to stimulate ideas. Providing creative teams with interesting snippets of information about the brand (its history, how it was made, how it is used, etc.) may help to provoke an advertising idea. Vivid and evocative descriptions of the target audience, and how they relate to the brand, can help to enthuse and interest creative teams. Analogies − comparing the brand with one in another market − can help to provide a feel for the brand's personality. The written brief should contain the following.

Background to the advertising problem

This firstly provides a brief summary of the current status of the brand or service − what it is, what it does, who uses it, where it stands in relation to competition, and so on. The extent to which such information is elaborated on depends on whether creative teams are working on a brand which is new to them, or familiar.

Secondly, this section provides creative people with an understanding of how we reached the advertising strategy, paying particular attention to any problems the brand may have which have led to a strategy change or modification.

Advertising strategy

The brief then contains the advertising strategy, although this may be elaborated on, especially in relation to the description of the target audience. It can be particularly useful to provide a 'pen-portrait' of the advertising target, giving the creative team a real feeling of a person with whom they are trying to communicate.

Mechanical requirement

The brief will obviously spell out exactly what is required in terms of intended media (TV/ Press/Outdoor etc.), the number of executions required and the degree of finish required at this stage. Timing and budgetary constraints will be indicated, together with any legal or Advertising Standards Authority restrictions.

The creative brief is critically important in the process of developing advertising. All the earlier effort is worth nothing if it is not given to creative people in the best form. It is the point at which all the previous research, analysis and thinking is focused to form the springboard from which advertising is developed.

3
Advertising that sells

How can we create an advertising idea that will be effective in the market-place?

This is the most important task in advertising.

Over the years we have learnt a lot of lessons at Leo Burnett from a consistent and regular analysis of advertising that has been effective.

That does not mean we can set out any fool-proof rules for people to follow. Every new advertising task is a new opportunity, but experience has taught us some basic disciplines to adopt, key questions to ask and which executional techniques to consider, so that we are likely to have a better chance of success than most.

Almost every success shows there is no substitute for thoroughness in approach and no substitute for imagination in creating thought-provoking ideas.

At its most basic, advertising is simply bringing a product and people together in an idea that is strongly branded.

When we try to evaluate an advertising idea we can ask questions about each component.

Of the product − what fundamental advantage are we offering over the competitors?

To the people we are targeting at − is our idea attracting, involving and motivating them?

On **branding** − have we done our best to ensure our ideas can be identified with the brand we are advertising?

Often all three components are very much a part of every execution. Sometimes the focus is clearly on the product, sometimes we depend on the use of people, and sometimes we rely heavily on a brand property. Knowing where to put the emphasis, and why, is critical in developing advertising ideas that are effective in the market-place.

Focus on the product

As a golden rule, the product component should always be considered first. After all, the prime aim of advertising is to establish a unique advantage for a product or service. And the best solution is to create a unique presentation of that advantage.

Given that belief, the most important technique you can use, especially on television, is demonstration. Demonstration shows your advantage. So, whenever you can show what a product can do well, show it — as often as you can.

There are many kinds of demonstrations.

Product explanation

Where you can explain a product advantage visually you have the strongest case for demonstration.

For example, a complicated idea can be simplified as we did with Mother's Pride bread. To show that each loaf of pre-wrapped white sliced bread contained as much protein as nine standard eggs, and as much energy value as five pints of milk, we simply showed that many eggs and that many pints of milk being taken out of a single loaf of Mother's Pride.

Side-by-side

These demonstrations which work as well in print as on television give you the chance to show your advantage in comparison with the competition. Generally, the simpler the comparison the better. As we did in a TV commercial which compared a can of Sandtex paint with an ordinary cheaper paint and stood it beside the can of Sandtex. Then we showed the cheaper paint cracking and peeling as it would over time.

Before and after

This is a technique where you demonstrate what happens before and after the use of a product. This is often the technique for cold and headache remedies. The secret of its success lies in the way you show the difference. The mistake is to give all the emphasis to the 'before'.

Torture tests

This is by far the most misused form of demonstration, where an extreme example sets out to prove a point. While you can show a car driving over a bed of nails to prove how tough the tyres are, it is essential that the viewers know the test is extreme. Otherwise there is the danger that the product is associated too easily with the need for extreme situations.

Product in action

This is the simplest type of demonstration. The product speaks for itself, as with many of the commercials we have produced for Austin Rover where we show the different cars put through their paces in tests and on the race track.

When the product in action provides a strong dramatic visual, look no further. You're on to a winner.

Showing the product in action is not restricted to television. For example with 3M Magic Tape we were able to demonstrate on posters that our tape could be written on or typed over while other tapes could not.

Food demonstrations

These are widely used in magazines but often overlooked for television. Food demonstrations on television are watched by women as avidly as they read recipes in magazines. They can show how new food products should be used and are also ideal for extending the usage of already established foods, as with most of the Crosse & Blackwell recipe series.

Simulated demonstrations

To demonstrate the product, you don't have to film the real thing. On the small television screen, simulated demonstrations can often be more dramatic than the real thing. For example, in a commercial for the Austin Mini we filled the screen with the word 'Mini' and allowed the dot over the first 'i' to speed around the screen going in and out of the letters to demonstrate the cheekiness and manoeuvrability of the real car.

Occasionally, you can best demonstrate a product advantage through analogy. This we did in a commercial for Mafu fly killers. All fly killers kill flies but Mafu has a deadly four-day residual effect. This we likened to the effect of a Venus fly-trap to show that even days later there was no escaping the power of Mafu. Before using analogy as a creative technique, be sure it is relevant and capable of creating an impact that other demonstrations cannot achieve.

That there are so many ways to demonstrate a product's advantage is not surprising. There is no more effective way to advertise a product.

If there's some advice we would pass on to those creating demonstrations for advertising, it would be this. Try to make the demonstration as simple as possible. Use close-ups wherever you can. Don't complicate the idea with too many trappings. Try to make every demonstration something that has never been used before. And once you've hit on a great demonstration go on using it as long as the advantage is yours.

In some commercials a demonstration is carried as a continuing visual proof of a product's advantage and can last for years and years, thus becoming a brand property in its own right. As with the shattering-glass device we use for Memorex tapes to register the theme: 'Is it live, or is it Memorex?'

Demonstrations also offer special advantages to the advertiser. With a demonstration the execution can rarely overshadow the product. And there's the added bonus that production costs are usually considerably less than with other techniques.

Product as hero

There are other techniques to focus on the product such as making the product the hero which we did in launching Nestle's Tip Top. We created a dancing can which poured its creamy topping on to different desserts, but this was still just as much a recipe demonstration using a strong executional technique.

The key to all advertising which puts the focus on the product is to dramatize the advantage it offers and the chances are that the best results will be some form of demonstration.

The use of people

There are two main uses of people for television advertising. Direct. And indirect.

The direct approach uses television as a person to person medium with someone talking directly to you.

The indirect approach uses television for the oldest dramatic technique of all – actors enacting a story.

As far as the direct approach is concerned you have a choice of presenters or testimonials from real people.

Presenters

Presenters are the obvious choice when you have genuine product news.

This approach depends largely on the convincingness of the presenter – especially when the news value is not very strong.

You can use spokesmen or spokeswomen and they can be experts or celebrities. Generally, celebrities are less convincing in shifting brand preference unless your product is part entertainment because celebrities are the most obviously paid performers.

The best presenters go beyond the message they have to deliver. They help build an image for the product. Which is why well-known personalities should be chosen to match the brand personality.

Perhaps the most dramatic sales results we have yet achieved in London came from the use of Daley Thompson, the Olympic and World Decathlon champion, to promote the energy giving properties of Lucozade (see Chapter 12). Within three months of the new advertising starting, the brand achieved its biggest sales jump ever and this for a brand that has been around for over 50 years.

Testimonials

Testimonials, using real people, are best deployed when product advantages are hard to show.

The point of most testimonials is to make an advertising claim believable.

The strength of this approach depends on the strength of

conviction that is put across.

The best testimonials capture that magic human moment that it is impossible to script for. It may be a laugh, a stutter, a shyness that is overcome, but it is a moment that endears the viewer to the person on the screen because you know it's real and spontaneous.

Given that most advertising is a studied, compressed form of communication in a wonderworld where nothing goes wrong, spontaneous testimony becomes a welcome change.

The most usual structure for testimonials is to take non-users who are claiming conversion to a brand.

But compelling commercials can also be made with people who are loyal to a brand as we did with the relaunch of Macleans. We simply showed young boys and girls telling us they all had one thing in common. 'We've never had a filling in our lives. And we've always used Macleans.'

Enacted stories

The indirect approach is all about enacted stories, where the viewer is the observer. Its great strength is that it involves people with the product.

Slice of life

There are several types of story structure but certainly the most misunderstood and misused by English advertisers and agencies is 'slice-of-life'.

While English television abounds with many successful situation comedies, few British creative people are able to adopt this technique for commercials. The best slice-of-life ideas are larger than life, almost closer to a French farce. They use eccentric characters and portray incidents that are exaggerated for entertainment. The key to these commercials is characterization and dialogue.

As a word of advice, slice-of-life ideas should not strive to be true to life. This is where they fall down.

Weak slice-of-life commercials are weak because they take themselves too seriously. Often they make the product seem too important for the story.

True-to-life stories

There are times when you can portray stories that are true to life. These are best used when the product can genuinely be presented as important to people. For example, a tyre commercial that shows you can avoid a serious accident or a public service campaign advocating 'Don't drink and drive'. As a maxim, if your story can be true to the product you can be true to life.

Playlets

The playlet technique leans more on story content than characterization and is usually better handled in Britain than slice-of-life. Here the story itself is more important than the characters. The secret is to build a dramatic story round the brand, as we have done for over 15 years with the man in black who, after an adventurous and dangerous escapade, delivers his box of Cadbury's Milk Tray.

Problem solution

The problem-solution approach works as well for creating stories as it does for product demonstrations. It is best used where a problem can be created to which your product is an ideal solution. The only danger with this approach is portraying too much problem and not enough solution. We produced some interesting problem-solution stories for Alka Seltzer where people were shown to be suffering from the effects of eating and drinking before building to the theme: 'Plink, Plink, Fizz. Oh what a relief it is.' Whenever this approach is used it is essential to come out strongly on the positive side to end the commercial.

Heart tuggers

One story technique which was developed by Creative Director Norman Muse, in our Chicago Agency, is aptly called by him the heart tugger. This is primarily an emotional story built around the product. It is ideal where children or family sentiment can be created around the brand, as with a pet food or greetings card. As a technique it can also provide great opportunities for print advertising photography.

Modern parables

This is more of an analogous story which is best left for well-established products where you are trying to get people to think of a product afresh. For less familiar products it is usually too indirect. We used this technique when we retold the stories of Caesar about to be stabbed in the back and the entry of the Wooden Horse of Troy to advertise *The Times*. They fitted well with our theme: 'Don't you wish you were better informed? Don't you wish you read *The Times*?'

Life style

This is more of a look-at-life approach where the product is shown to fit a particular life style. It is best used when a product is evaluated on a social rather than a functional basis, as with most soft drinks. In this case it is essential that the life style depicted is genuinely liked or aspired to by a large enough group of people.

Fantasy stories

This is one of the most fertile areas for ideas, particularly if you can portray a generally-held fantasy involving the product. This we did very successfully in a beer commercial for McEwan's Export by dramatizing what was almost every beer drinker's fantasy: starting a relationship with an attractive barmaid.

Brand properties

Every product or people technique should try to use an idea or campaign that results in identification with the brand.

Techniques which ignore branding contribute more to wasted advertising money than anything else. The fact that at least two-thirds of all advertising is still misidentified is something that we at Leo Burnett work hard to overcome.

Some products, which have little to differentiate them from

their competition other than the name and the pack, require advertising that relies almost exclusively on building a strong brand image.

In this case, the idea must not only try to add value to the brand, it must also be capable of building a strong brand preference over the competition — a tall order, indeed.

As a goal for all products, we should try to build into the advertising some form of branding memory trigger or brand property.

At Leo Burnett we work hard to create strong brand properties. Sometimes they are the focal point of the advertising. Other times they are simply a way of integrating the idea and the brand.

Here then is a list of techniques through which brand properties can be created.

Animation

This is recognized to be especially effective for appealing to children and has been widely used in the Kellogg children's cereal characters created by our Leo Burnett partners in Chicago, like Tony the Tiger and Snap, Crackle and Pop.

Animation can also be used to appeal to parents and children as with the Smurfs which were used to build continuous brand loyalty for National Benzole stations.

As a technique, animation can even be used to appeal to men, as we showed when we translated a masculine newspaper cartoon style into the rugged Grousebeater characters who would drink nothing but McEwan's lager.

Animation can further be used to simplify complex ideas. It can also treat abstract or distasteful subjects in a way that is acceptable for family viewing at home.

Whatever the style, the secret of animation lies in creating an individual personality for the brand being advertised.

Continuing characters

These, by their nature, can help build a long-term campaign for a brand.

They can be eccentric characters in slice-of-life campaigns or animated characters which become part of advertising folklore as with the Jolly Green Giant.

Brand symbols

As with celebrities the power of a symbol depends on its relevance.

The greatest strength of a symbol is in registering the brand identity.

Few campaigns with strongly used brand symbols are misidentified.

One of the strongest and longest-running campaigns Leo Burnett developed in the UK was actually built around a symbol. This is the advertising for Strongbow cider which has used the arrow as symbol of strength for over twelve years and helped to take its brand share from 11 per cent to 29 per cent over that period. In this case the symbol was used to build a strong brand personality.

Music

Music can be used to reinforce a message, but it can also lower the ability of a commercial to be remembered.

There are two main types of music for commercials.

Theme music. This can increase a mood or emotions but is not always as strongly related to the brand as it should be. Originally scored music has a much better chance of becoming a brand property while a well-known tune can too often remind people of the tune and not of the brand. This puts more onus on the visual content to be highly branded.

Jingles. A good jingle will always increase brand memorability. It's what jingles are about.

The ideal music is that which, over time, registers the brand almost instantly in people's minds and the longer a piece of music is used the stronger the brand connection.

A musical. There is another whole use of music which is more akin to a stage production. This involves people singing and dancing usually in large-scale expensive productions. They should only be necessary for undifferentiated brands where entertainment value is important. Too often they are an excuse for having no strong selling idea.

Vignettes

These are a series of cameos usually repeating the same idea with different people.

They are an ideal structure where the advertising idea has been crystallized into a short simple message.

The extra repetitions of message and vignettes work that much harder when they are totally focused on the same point.

This was a key element in the successful relaunch commercial we created for Body Mist deodorant. Here we showed the problem three times over of people not wanting to stand close to someone, then, after introducing the product, we visualized the theme: 'Stand close with Body Mist.'

Multi-cuts

Here the commercial creates a kaleidoscope impression generally with a lot of fast-cutting visuals edited to the tempo of a modern upbeat piece of music.

This fast-cutting technique is better suited to a younger, modern appeal, but is still best judged by its branding ability.

As with musical commercials, there is a danger of the production overwhelming the message. It is essential that the overall impression is single-minded even if the execution seems complicated.

Special techniques

There is always the temptation to use some novel technique particularly when creative people are striving for originality.

The acid test is whether or not the technique takes over from the brand.

Only use special techniques when it drives home the message as well as the branding.

For example, the use of slow motion for a fabric softener dropping on to clothes is a wonderful way to depict softness.

Slogans

Most great advertising campaigns have a slogan. It isn't essential to have one, and there are many campaigns that do not.

As a discipline it is always worthwhile setting out to come up with a telegraphic set of words which summarize a campaign idea. If eventually you don't use those specific words at least you will have condensed your thinking and the chances of people understanding your advertising message are higher.

It is worth registering that slogans work far faster on television and radio than on posters and even on posters slogans work much faster than in print advertising.

Here are just a few of the best known slogans from Leo Burnett, London:

And all because the lady loves Milk Tray.

Strongbow. Strong as your thirst.

Flake. The crumbliest flakiest milk chocolate in the world.

Metro. A British car to beat the world.

See Sanyo then decide.

McEwan's Export. The one you don't down in one.

Lucozade aids recovery.

Did you Maclean your teeth today?

What makes for an effective television commercial?

We have concentrated very much on the different techniques available but there are still a few telling ways of evaluating an advertising idea at the storyboard stage or at the first showing of the commercial.

Here are just a few questions to ask:

■ Does the commercial tell the full story in pictures? We must never forget that television is primarily a visual medium.

■ Is there a key visual which dramatizes the main selling idea?

- Is there a magic moment in the commercial, something that lifts it out of the ordinary?

- Is the opening attention-getting? Commercials can never build attention. You can only hope to hold on to viewers.

- Is the rest of the commercial involving?

- Is there a pay-off?

- Is the commercial memorably branded?

- Does the tone reflect the brand personality?

What makes for an effective print advertisement?

A lot of the techniques we've discussed apply as much to print as to television advertising, but there are a number of questions that can be asked of any press layout to check its likely effectiveness.

- Is there impact? Impact for print is twice as important as relevance. That is not an excuse to cheat people into an advertisement, but research shows time and time again that most advertising in print is passed over. In fact less than 10 per cent of press advertising is noticed by anyone. Therefore every print advertisement needs stopping power.

- Does it flag the prospects? The more select the audience the more they should be mentioned in the headline.

- If you're relying on the headline, is it telegraphic and newsy? The ideal is a telegram from the heart.

- If it's a copy advertisement, is the copy readable? Too many headlines are made difficult to read by using all capital letters. Too many advertisements have long copy that is reversed out and impossible to read.

- If it's a picture advertisement, is the picture big enough? Too often the emphases of words and pictures are too equal to give proper emphasis to either.

- Does the picture tell a story? Putting a story appeal in pictures attracts high attention, as do pictures of personalities, babies and animals.

- Is the advertisement properly branded? You should at least be able to tell at a glance what it is you are advertising or have very good reasons why not.

What makes for an effective poster?

There are very few questions to ask of a poster. Most times people have only three seconds to notice it.

- Is there a big idea?

- Have you dared to be bold?

- Does its impact stop you?

- Is it simple? The fewer the words the better.

For years we have run outstanding posters for Perrier. Most of the early posters were only 4 and 16 sheet sizes. Interestingly we rarely used more than two words per poster:

H2Eau
Eau-la-la
Eau Revoir
N'eau Calories
Picasseau
Bistreau

What makes for effective radio advertising?

Radio can be the most creative medium of all. It forces the listener to use his own imagination, to picture thoughts in his own mind.

Sadly, too little radio stretches the imagination.

Radio is also a slower medium and can never be as compressed as television. It needs a single-minded approach.

At the same time radio as a medium is very easy to switch off in the mind, so it doesn't help to have a single voice droning away.

Another overlooked factor is that radio is very much a news medium and can be used for very topical messages.

Here are some of the key questions to ask of any radio idea:

- Does it flag the audience quickly? Not everyone listening can be your target.

- Do you mention the brand early? People's imagination can quickly take them down a different road from the way you want to go.

- Is the key thought clearly put across?

- Is there a memorable sound? Radio is ideal for music memory triggers.

- Is there sufficient variety of sounds or voices to keep the interest going?

- Is there a summary or take away of the main idea?

- And finally, could we stretch the imagination further?

Take a step back

There is no easy way to determine if an advertising idea can be effective. It takes a lot of hard work to get to the final, simple solution.

Nevertheless, there should always be a time for everyone closely involved with any advertising idea when they take a step back to review the work from a distance.

At this point it is best to repeat some fundamental questions.

If we are focusing our idea on the product, have we a strong product advantage? Is our case convincing? Is it convincing enough to encourage people to switch brands?

If we are making use of people, have we a strong emotional appeal? Is our advertising motivating? Has it the power to pull prospects from other brands?

As for branding, have we created a strong enough brand property? Does it lock our idea into our brand? Does the overall image add value to the brand?

Overall, have we produced an idea that will encourage enough people to switch brands?

For most advertising at Leo Burnett, that is our goal. Brand preference advertising.

4

What's the big idea?

Some sixty years ago, before television, an eminent American copywriter, Claude Hopkins, described his job as 'salesmanship in print'.

It is a useful definition. Advertising is selling. And good advertising works like a good salesman.

First he works out what his product has to offer that is of the most interest to the potential purchaser. Then he sets about drawing attention to this in a way that sets him apart from his rivals.

He does this in the most imaginative, rewarding way he can devise – so the message is more likely to be remembered, and the customer is also more likely to think well of the seller and his product. The good salesman never underestimates the value of goodwill.

Finally, once he's got his act together (and it can take a good deal of experimentation, a lot of trial and error) he uses it again and again and again. Of course, he refreshes it from time to time to stop it getting boring or stale. But he keeps the basic underlying 'sell' intact.

It is this aspect of advertising, the value of consistent, long-running campaigns and what gives them their legs, that we shall discuss in this chapter.

Why does Leo Burnett look for the big, enduring idea?

The answer depends on whether you believe in the cumulative effect; whether you believe in building brands or simply in advertising products; and whether you believe that advertising is in itself something with a life and personality that can grow, develop its own character and evolve.

The value of repetition — and its problems

There can be no doubt that the more you repeat something the more likely it is to be remembered. Repetition of the selling message is one of the basic tenets of advertising. If we can afford it, we do it.

The problem is that if the message is repeated parrot-fashion enough times people become blind to it — the wallpaper effect.

You admire it when it's new, but it soon disappears. So after a while you need to change your message.

At this point you can either prepare an advertisement that has nothing in common with its predecessor, or you can produce one that has a link, some common element. That's the difference between a series of 'one-offs' and a campaign.

If you believe in the value of repetition then it must make sense that you should repeat or echo as many elements as possible, even if you can't repeat the whole advertisement effectively. Nowhere is this more evident than in the cluttered multi-product confectionery market, in which long-running campaigns have maintained the predominance of brands such as Cadbury's Flake and Milk Tray when many other products have come, temporarily prospered, and equally quickly disappeared from the market.

If your advertising problem is one that can be solved only by a series of short-term, different tactical messages, then 'one-offs' are what you want. By definition your message should be different every time.

But if your product does not change its fundamental nature — if its basic promise remains the same — then consistency in your advertising message must be a virtue.

Turning the product into a brand

Advertising is far and away the most powerful way a product can say something about itself, can express its personality.

Advertising is the product's clothes, its accent, its sense of humour, its seriousness, its masculinity or femininity, its honesty, its zaniness, its class, its sexiness or homeliness.

If a product turned up each year looking different and saying something different about itself you'd be confused. You wouldn't know what to think of it. But if a product presents the same face, same character, the same promise year in, year out, you know exactly where you stand and what to expect. It is this continuity of character that turns products into brands. It makes them familiar, friendly, comfortable faces — someone you understand, you have confidence in.

Advertising has a life of its own

Years ago someone at Guinness said: 'We make three products — bottled Guinness, draught Guinness and advertising.' The advertising you do both reflects the product and reflects upon it. If the advertising is 'good' in the consumers' eyes, then the product is likely to be good, too — until proven otherwise.

It is this independent 'life' that makes the final argument in favour of the big, enduring idea; the expansive campaign.

When you see a good new advertisement, you think: 'That's interesting, I like that.' It makes an impression. When you see a series of new advertisements with a common theme, you have a deeper impression. The advertising immediately has a breadth, a stature, that a single advertisement cannot aspire to.

Give it a good start

The results of this for the advertiser are numerous. You immediately make a stronger impression for your product. And not just on the consumer — it also affects your sales force, your shareholders, your factory, and your distributors. Here's something you're serious about. It's not just a one-off, a flash in the pan.

And it's usually a good investment to produce more than one execution (to use more than one medium, maybe) right from the kick-off. Of course this is more expensive, but it usually pays off.

A potentially strong campaign can wither on the vine because the initial execution has not been followed up quickly enough with another. Consequently the campaign has lacked substance, there has been no commitment, there has been no encouragement for the idea to take wing and fly. For example, on Perrier, the original 'Eau la la' advertisement not only communicated the product in a meaningful and impactful way, but established a pattern for a quick introduction of a whole series of related executions which rapidly built the image of this brand.

Watch it grow

Once the campaign is well and truly under way, the big, enduring idea really comes into its own. It feeds upon itself and grows in the mind of the consumer. People look forward to the next subject and greet it as an old friend in an attractive new outfit. It reminds. It reinforces. It reveals slightly different facets of its character, all the while growing in stature; and, above all, stamping an unequivocal promise for the brand it represents.

Eventually it takes its place in the vernacular of the people at which it is aimed. It turns up in the nation's small-talk, its jokes, its football chants, the editorial columns of the papers, the pages of Punch, the Morecambe and Wise Show. And each time it does, it gains in strength. Driving deeper and deeper into the national consciousness. If the underlying thought behind the advertising idea has the integrity it should have, even parodies of it will serve to cement the product and its promise.

Other advantages of long-running campaigns

Once an advertising theme has been strongly implanted in people's minds, peripheral advantages come into play.

Obviously you need fewer exposures for the advertising to trigger the desired response in the consumer than if your message is totally new and unfamiliar. Analyses of **tracking studies** (measuring the degree of advertising recall at regular intervals over extended periods) show that, with the same number of exposures, new advertisements in a familiar campaign tend to score much better than those after a complete change. So well-established advertising ideas can be more economical in pure media cost. (But beware of starving the goose that lays the golden eggs. Long-running ideas can get stale without fresh injections of interest.)

A less tangible but perhaps more valuable economy that comes from the long-running advertising campaign stems from the fact that you do not have to spend time and energy devising new advertising themes every year.

The creation of a new campaign takes up huge chunks of both agency and client man-hours. It is costly in research. It takes considerable management involvement. And, though it is nearly always exciting and rewarding, it demands considerable input and concentration − a process that can take your eyes off other vital aspects of the marketing.

How do you set about creating a long-running campaign?

As with any successful advertising, it all starts with the thinking you do before you put creative pen to paper. Although the most obvious and recognizable attributes of any long-running campaigns are the substantial, developable, repeatable creative elements, what gives it its underlying strength and relevance is the strategy on which it is based.

If there is one single thread that runs through any successful long-running campaign, it is that the creative content is totally in tune with and identified with the brand. There is a truth, an integrity, a unity between the brand and its advertising. The one reinforces the other, both rationally and emotionally − genuine synergy that grows geometrically year after year.

The search is on

The most frequent question you hear when you are looking for an advertising idea with longevity is: 'Is it campaignable?'. It is much better to ask: 'Is it good advertising?':

■ Is it true to the product? Does it fit the brand's nature and positioning?

■ Is the idea distinctive? different? motivating?

■ Is it a genuine idea, and not just a technique? Does it fire the imagination?

■ Is the advertisement illuminating and rewarding?

■ Is the execution simple? attention-getting? memorable?

If you can answer yes to these questions, you have good advertising and the chances are overwhelming that you will be able to campaign it.

It doesn't always happen overnight

Patience can be a virtue when you are seeking the great, enduring advertising idea. Even when you have the strategy sewn up and you have a campaignable idea, it may still lack the distinctive element that will turn solid advertising into something on a different plane altogether.

For example, perhaps the single most successful advertising idea of all time, the Marlboro Cowboy, was a long time in being born.

The birth pangs of an advertising legend

To put it in perspective, Marlboro was the first filter cigarette to be launched in the United States — way back in the 1930s when untipped cigarettes were the norm. It was very much a woman's cigarette, and it did reasonably well. But when sales reached a plateau, Leo Burnett, Chicago, rethought the strategy.

It went like this: Marlboro is a woman's cigarette. Men will never smoke a woman's cigarette. Men smoke more than women. So your sales potential is severely limited. Therefore, make Marlboro a man's cigarette.

It was a courageous strategic decision that was to revolutionize the brand, and America's and eventually the world's smoking habits.

To change Marlboro's image so drastically required an equally dramatic change in advertising. Like so many far-reaching marketing and advertising decisions it appears simple, even naive, in retrospect. But there can be no denying the boldness and imagination of the people who made the change — and, above all, their faith in the power of advertising.

They decided to sell flavour in the cigarette, masculinity in the smoker. To do this, they devised the simple advertising idea of showing men who demanded real satisfaction from their cigarette smoking Marlboro.

They showed a stevedore, a miner, a truckdriver, a diver. And so on. One face among this gallery was the cowboy.

Once more with hindsight, it is obvious that the cowboy has all the attributes of fact and folklore (bolstered by a thousand 'westerns') to be the ultimate man's and woman's man. But at

The Flake girl in 1962
(see p. 103 for 1982)

consistent theme that has run for over twenty five years. It is constantly up-dated, but always retains the original feel and mood. There have been occasional minor changes to the copy to emphasize this or that aspect. A tactical and successful innovation (see Chapter 9) has not weakened our belief in our basic execution. The only significant change this has seen in a quarter of a century has been the addition of music. Even that has remained essentially unaltered since it was first introduced. Only the singers and arrangements change to keep up with current trends.

Tone of voice

Long-running campaigns can, however, depend totally on tone and consistency of approach rather than on specific executional characteristics. Volvo does not rely on a single idea. It does not have a slogan. Over the years it has not had a standard look or typeface. There has simply been a persistent and all-pervasive projection (in both visual and copy) of the sound middle-class virtues of an ultra-safe, well-built, Swedish motor-car.

The success of the campaign has been its total consonance with the brand and its seamless sense of style.

The brand device

Leo Burnett's advertising for Strongbow, on the other hand, has made extensive and consistent use of a very specific executional element − a brand device, an audio-visual metaphor. The Strongbow arrows have become synonymous with the brand, to such an extent that if you play a tape with the sound of two arrows twanging and thumping into wood you get the Pavlovian reaction, 'Strongbow'.

The potency of this is not, however, that it conjures up the brand name so unerringly. It is that it is so resonant of the product's characteristics. It is the embodiment of Strongbow − a clean, strong, clear, sharp, tangy, true pint.

The Strongbow arrows
selling bottles (1969)

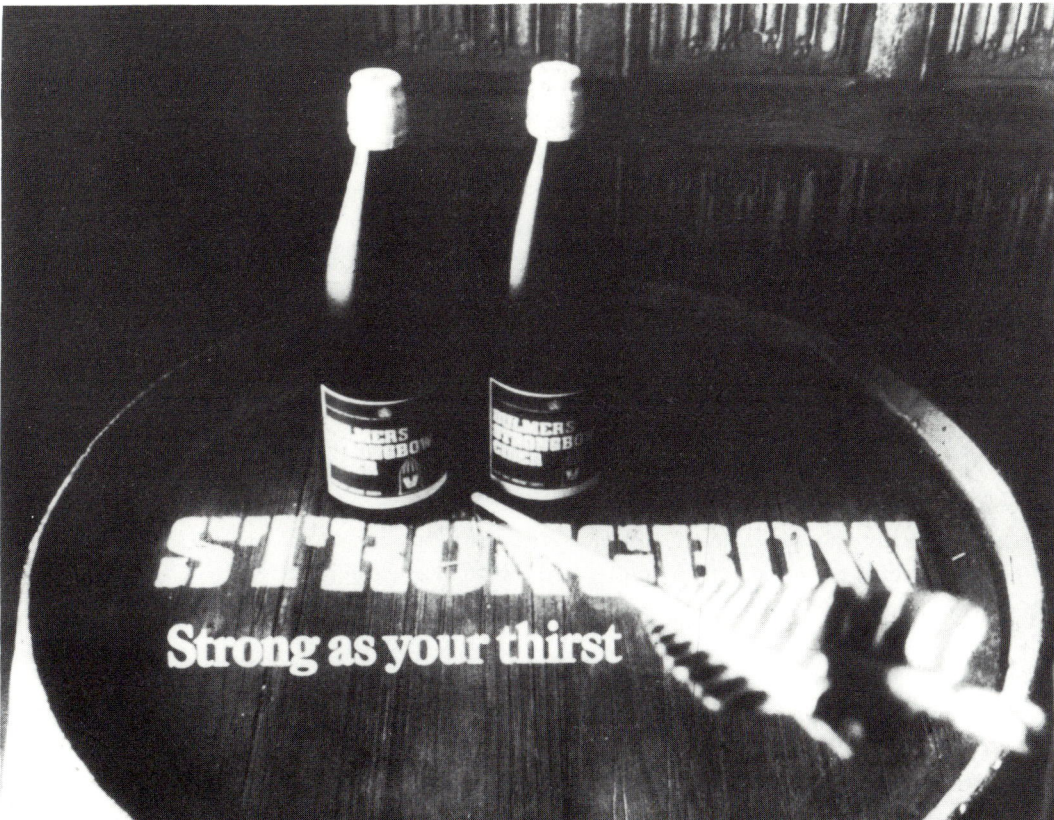

STRONGBOW
Strong as your thirst

Characters

Taking this inter-relationship of the brand and its advertising to the ultimate, there have been many examples where the brand itself (or a character representing the brand) has provided the advertising idea.

The Jolly Green Giant and his Garden in the Valley is a classic example. Originally the Green Giant was simply the symbol of the Minnesota Packing Company. He was then a dwarf rather than a giant — a Pan figure, a symbol of Nature. Leo Burnett made him larger than life and projected him so powerfully that the company even changed its name to Green Giant. That campaign, started in the 1930s, is still running.

Other long-running campaigns have created their own characters. It is a simple and obvious way to provide potential longevity. Once more in the United States, Leo Burnett created Charlie the Tuna for Starkist. Charlie was the Tuna doomed to perpetual disappointment in his efforts to get canned by Starkist. He simply wasn't up to standard.

The list of these advertising characters is virtually endless. The PG Chimps, Speedy Alka Seltzer, the Dulux Dog, Captain Birds Eye, Oxo's Katy, Tony the Tiger, the Marlboro Cowboy....

They don't all work in exactly the same way, but they all have one thing in common — someone or something to act as a focus for the kind of human attributes we can all identify with and relate to in a more intimate and acceptable way than we could with a tablet, a packet of fish fingers, a tea-bag or a can of sweet corn.

They literally bring the brand to life for us.

How long can a long-running campaign run?

The story is told of the advertiser who, on seeing his commercial for the umpteenth time in the agency's cinema, suggested that it was getting worn out and that it was time for a change. The agency's powers of tact and diplomacy were exercised to the full in reminding the client that the campaign had not yet even broken.

The client had seen so many scripts, storyboards, animatics, rough cuts, **doubleheads** and final prints that he was bored with it before the public had seen it.

The truth is that clients (and agencies) often get disenchanted with advertising and hanker for a change long before the public do.

It takes many exposures of a soundly based, imaginatively written, well produced advertisement for it to wear thin. (Conversely, if an advertisement is dull, shoddily produced and bereft of reward, even one exposure is one too many.)

By extension, a powerful, expansive, rich campaign can run and run for as long as the underlying selling message continues to be relevant.

When do you change?

The glib answer is: 'when the campaign stops working'. But the simple fact is that, without doubt, more great advertising properties have been abandoned prematurely than have lingered on to the detriment of the brand.

If an advertising idea has true underlying strength, is faithful to the brand and has captured the public imagination (and all great long-running campaigns have these characteristics), then it is liable to be extremely resilient. It will almost certainly respond to good husbandry and intelligent efforts to keep it alive when under threat.

Strongbow is a good example. The arrows have carried the brand successfully through many strategies in the sixteen years since their creation. They launched the brand in bottles. They introduced cans. They introduced draught. They were used to recommend Strongbow as a change from lager. Now they are being successfully used to strengthen Strongbow's position as a regular, everyday pint alongside bitter.

On the other hand, there may be campaigns which continue to deliver the right long-term strategic positioning for the brand, but which do not wholly meet short-term needs. This was the case with Cadbury's Flake (see Chapter 9), for which the solution was to augment the long-running campaign with a tactical message on a separate execution, rather than depart from the well-proven successful formula.

Obviously campaigns do eventually wear out, strategies do change and the advertising idea cannot always make that leap. So campaigns do have to be changed. But when in doubt, stick it out − always remember this: a great advertising idea is an invaluable property. Often it takes years to find, to establish, to harness and hone. You throw it away at your peril. Your first thought should not be 'How can we change it?' but 'How can we keep it?'.

It is said that a client once asked Rosser Reeves (head of Ted Bates in New York at the time) why there were 100 agency people working on his business when he had run the same campaign for years. 'One to write the advertising, 99 to stop you changing it' was the answer.

It is undoubtedly true that the quickest and most visible way for a client brand-man to make his mark (in the two years he has before he moves on) is to leave his imprint on the advertising for his brand. At the very least he's likely to question the current campaign and actively try to find weaknesses. In attempting to shore up these 'weak spots' the delicate balance of the entire campaign can be damaged.

The Strongbow arrows selling draught (1983)

At the worst, the ambitious brand-man will try to leave behind him his own, totally new, campaign.

It takes a good deal of maturity and self-confidence in the brand-man to realize that, often, the biggest contribution he can make to the brand while it is in his temporary custody is to leave the advertising idea alone.

You can't afford to be complacent. You can kill a great campaign by neglect as easily as by interference. It must be kept fresh and alive. It must develop, however subtly. Marlboro, Strongbow, Flake ... all the great long-term campaigns have done this.

Do long-running campaigns work?

The answer is, of course, that they do work. They wouldn't be long-running if they didn't work.

The Marlboro Cowboy has taken the Marlboro brand from seventh position in the United States to first position in the world over forty years.

'All because the lady loves Milk Tray' has taken Milk Tray from the number three chocolate assortment in 1968 to number one today.

Twenty five years of Flake advertising has helped build a £40 million brand.

The real question is: 'would a series of one-offs work better?' And the answer to that, for the vast majority of products, must surely be 'no'.

It all comes back to cumulative effect. The more you repeat a message the more likely it is to be remembered. The more flesh you put on 'an idea the more it comes to life. The more dimensions you add, the greater the stature.

You start building a brand rather than advertising a product. You add value to it. You provide consistency, continuity, confidence, character, charisma.

Imagine you have a load of bricks. Use them one by one and you can do lots of useful things. You can use them as doorstops, paperweights, bookends. You can strike matches on one, block up a rabbit hole with another. You can even use one to bung through a jeweller's window. Lots and lots of things. Put them together and you build a house.

5

Producing advertising efficiently

The advertiser sees the production of advertising mainly as a cost. The agency sees it mainly as an opportunity to do great work. These viewpoints need to be reconciled.

Both sides are, of course, agreed that the financial objective is to divide the total advertising budget into production and media spends which together have the maximum effect on the target. One mistake would be to allocate too much to production and waste money which would be better spent on showing a good, relevant advertisement more often. Another mistake would be to skimp on production and finish with an advertisement which just did not do the job.

Both are also agreed that you cannot simply equate production spend with effectiveness. There are examples of cheaply made but sales-effective advertising, though in general we get what we pay for. There are also examples of apparent cost-saving which is counter-productive.

Finally, both the advertiser and Leo Burnett want a way of making production decisions which is free from hassle and misunderstandings. From our wide experience we have production guidelines which achieve this, which balance economy and creative enthusiasm. We use our understanding of industry averages (in cost and quality), but we can also suggest departures from these norms.

The production budget

Overall industry information provides a basis against which the plans for individual advertisements and campaigns can be assessed.

Production accounts for somewhat less than 15 per cent of total spending in the two main media. This means that an advertiser with a total budget of £1 million spends about £850,000 on the cost of showing the advertisement (television time and newspaper space costs, for example) and on average less than £150,000 to make the advertisements physically (Table 5.1).

Table 5.1
Simple breakdown of advertising costs

	TV	Press (display)
Production (£m)	108	154
Total expenditure (£m)	928	1105
Production as percentage of total expenditure	12	14

Source: Advertising Association, 1982

The percentages in Table 5.1 conceal great variations. In Leo Burnett in 1982 we incurred production costs on sixty five major brands. The largest group of brands fell in the range 10 to 14 per cent spent on production, typical of the industry figures, and our overall average was 12 per cent. The spread was, however, very wide, and only twenty two of the sixty five were in the 'average' range. For twenty five brands the amount was low, 9 per cent or less. These tended to be long-running campaigns, or those for which we made a film the previous year and which we are still using. For eighteen brands the production spend was above average, and for eight it was over 40 per cent of the total spend. These tended to be launches, or had low total budgets.

Hence there is certainly no magic percentage figure to set as a production budget. It cannot be stated that given a £1 million budget above the line, production costs 'should be' £150,000. It is possible to fix such a level in the first very rough financial plan. Often common sense and experience will guide us to a first guess at a figure different from 15 per cent – much higher, for example, for a TV area launch, for such a product is expected later to go national; or much lower if we already have a proven commercial we intend to go on running.

Once we have such a figure, it should become part of our financial brief. The brief is not a commitment – it is a first shot at a plan which both partners query and modify together. We are agreeing only on an estimate. Either side can recommend changing it, with good reasons.

The advantage of this method is that a copywriter does not sit down in front of his typewriter with extravagant ideas about the advertisement he is going to write. It is when the script is written that the cash register starts to ring: a cast of thousands, or a voiceover; an exotic location and elaborate set, or a tabletop; material for one sixty second and several thirty second sequences, or for one at twenty seconds – these are all important decisions.

No one pretends that such a decision is easy, or purely financial. The real effectiveness of an advertisement is hard enough to measure even when it exists in rough form – we would say it is impossible to measure. When it is only an idea, it is clearly impossible to evaluate except by judgement.

Nevertheless, the advertiser should be ready to discuss, with an open mind, an advertising idea which goes over budget. It may be in this way that a breakthrough will be made.

So to fix a production budget as part of the advertising brief is not a straightjacket, it is a proposal for discussion. More and more advertisers are moving this way and it is a key step in reducing costs and in removing misunderstandings. It should be emphasized that setting a budget in advance never means doing production on the cheap. That is a recipe for disaster. As Leo Burnett said: 'The bitter taste of poor quality remains long after the sweet taste of low price has been forgotten'. What it does mean is writing an advertising campaign with an awareness of any budgetary constraints.

As a result maximum attention can then be directed both to writing and to choosing the production technique in the full knowledge of total affordability – and knowing the amount of exposure the campaign is likely to get, that is, the first shot at the media plan. Many good ideas will work only if they are seen sufficiently often.

The larger the budget, the smaller in general the production ratio should be. You do not necessarily need twice as many advertisements for a budget of £2 million as you do for a budget of £1 million. A small budget usually requires low-cost production, if not a low spend, to enable reasonable media cover and frequency to be achieved. For a low budget, a simple idea that works at one or two exposures is usually required.

For example, in the early 1970s an introductory advertise-ment for Cadbury's Old Jamaica was produced with all the appearances of a major outdoor location but actually using a tiny set in a small studio on a minuscule production cost out of a total advertising spend of £10,000, including media. Both the quality of the commercial and its sales results were good enough to warrant subsequent national transmission.

On the other hand, the successful implementation of many creative solutions requires a more extensive and time-consuming production programme. At today's rates it is not unusual for the total cost of television production to go over £200,000, particularly when it is planned to produce a number of films, including possibly fairly long versions for trade and PR purposes.

In these cases, it is critical that detailed costs are properly estimated and monitored against specific production opportunities.

The example summarized in Table 5.2 covered a studio shoot lasting five days, and resulted in four TV commercials. The production company element consists of many different items. In this example, the largest costs were for the lengthy hire and set building of the studio, £28,815; directors' and camera crew salaries, £22,500; art department salaries and costs for props, £11,430; and optical charges including end film animation, £11,520.

	£
Pre-production experimentation	1,322
Production company	131,178
Artistes	3,500
Music	7,500
Titles/logos artwork	500
Showprints (for all regions)	6,142
Cassette transfers	600
Agency commission	26,606
Total	**£177,348**

Table 5.2
Itemized costs on a major
TV production

The advertising idea

The strategy determines what the final advertising will be, in that it defines the consumer benefit. It should also indicate the overall tone of voice best suited to deliver this specific message. For example, the advertising may have to convey emotional or factual points. The style of advertising used to speak to the target may be vibrant and exciting or relaxed and laid-back.

As a rule, simple demonstrations of a simple product benefit are usually cheaper to produce than an emotional sell or complex idea.

For example, in Table 5.3 are shown two theoretical strategies for an identical chocolate bar — the difference in the strategies being in the benefit, the tone and the guidelines. Product and target audiences are the same.

	Strategy A	Strategy B
Product	Chocolate	Chocolate
Target audience	All adults	All adults
Benefit	Increased size	Heavenly taste
Tone	Factual	Optimistic and aspirational
Executional guidelines	Demonstrate the benefit	Outdoors
	No people	Summery
		Mouth-watering

Table 5.3
Alternative theoretical strategies for chocolate bar

In the case of strategy A, it is clear that a very simple factual demonstration of the benefit, the product's size, is all that is required. If TV is to be the medium, then a simple tabletop setting without people and probably lasting only twenty seconds. The result — a very simple and inexpensive film.

With strategy B, however, we have to communicate taste, always a more difficult thing; and heavenly taste at that, even more difficult. It means people for sure. But also, it probably means people outdoors in a beautiful atmospheric type of film, requiring a top-class director and lighting cameraman. Weather will be very important; therefore we may have to go abroad. Weather insurance may also be sensible. The result — an expensive production.

So if there is a tight budget it is essential that we are aware of this before creating advertising. We must check that the advertising strategy and the advertising idea are feasible within the draft production budget.

Production considerations
People costs

Developing the advertising strategy into an execution will have implications on the size of the cast.

The number and type of models obviously determine this cost. Recently this element has become a more significant part of the overall budget. This is particularly so on TV, where repeat fees have recently escalated, and may continue to increase. There is therefore pressure to keep costs down. Our experience has revealed some important opportunities.

First, only use stars when they are considered to be absolutely essential to the effectiveness of the commercial. Whilst we have several examples where they have been used successfully, such as John Cleese for General Accident and Terry Scott for Cadbury's Curly Wurly, personalities can be extremely expensive and may be troublesome (and where they are reasonable their agents may not be!). But equally, do not reject a star solely on grounds of economy.

Second, keep the number of featured artists down to a minimum.

Third, investigate whether it is better to buy out the artists rather than pay repeat fees.

Finally, cost out the repeat fees on a yearly basis *before* the film is made.

The media to be used

Quite obviously the cost of production will vary considerably depending on whether it is for TV, radio, cinema, poster, press, in black and white or in colour.

Although there are extreme budgetary circumstances in which certain media will be automatically ruled out, new opportunities for lower-cost, affordable, yet still good quality executions are on the increase. In television these may be related to the emergence of new media such as Channel 4, or from improved technology such as video. In press, publishers are continually striving to offer both better reproduction and improved timing, and the whole of the printing industry is experiencing the increasing benefits of computerized applications. For the majority of brands, the cost of production is unlikely to be the major determinant in the media decision. More important is the early consideration of the most efficient production process to exploit fully the potential of the media chosen, by achieving the best balance between creative effectiveness and overall campaign cost and performance.

Production methods

If the production ratio seems high, look at other methods of production that could deliver the same number of advertise-ments to the same strategy, but at a significant saving. For example, in the case of colour press, drawn artwork is often cheaper than photography. And in the case of film, animation is usually cheaper than live action.

The number of advertisements

The products which tend to have the lowest production ratios are those with long-running campaigns. These campaigns do not have to produce new advertisements every year, and frequently they can re-introduce those from the past and re-run them. For example, Cadbury, in 1983, is re-using a Flake commercial (in rotation with other films) that was shot in 1973. One of the great advantages of having a real enduring advertising property is that the longer it lasts the harder it works.

The brands which tend to have the highest production ratios are those which have a new campaign each year. There are two main reasons for frequently changing campaigns.

The first is the type of product. Some product categories require frequent relaunches, reformulations, repackaging. This makes it much more difficult to create and continue with a long-term enduring idea.

The second is the difficulty of finding an advertising idea which is strong enough to be an enduring long-term property. And even these recognized successes are under continuous pressure for change, sometimes for no better reason than for 'change's sake'.

Degree of quality

One of the most obvious ways of ensuring that production costs are kept to a minimum is to agree at the outset the production standard required. This can vary widely, depending on the media and the product.

Clearly, if replacement exhaust systems are to be advertised in the black and white local press, then it is not necessary to spend the sort of money on full-colour photography and artwork which is required for a high-class perfume advertised in Vogue. Put like this the point is obvious; but in practice money can frequently be saved by ensuring, at the outset, that everyone understands the budgetary restraints.

The creative department of any top agency expects to aim for superb quality, both in idea and execution. If they are not fully aware of budgetary constraints before the advertising idea is conceived, then there is the risk that ideas will be produced that cannot be afforded, or cost more money than was necessary.

Timing

The most common reason for spending excessive amounts of money on production nowadays is shortage of time. Less and less is being allowed, both for advertising development and advertising production. Some of the haste cannot be avoided, or more accurately may appear to be reasonable. However, when plenty of time is built into the plan, allowing for all eventualities during the course of a campaign's development and production, however difficult this may be in the context of the total marketing plan, the risk of spending more money unnecessarily is considerably decreased.

In the past it was not uncommon to allow a year or more for the development of a TV campaign, from brief to on-air; though for most products this may now appear to be unrealistic. Lack of time when it comes to actual production has two distinct risks.

The first is of losing quality because there is insufficient time to polish the idea, both pre- and post-production.

The second is the risk of spending money unnecessarily. Without proper time it is virtually impossible to book the technicians and artists really wanted. the choice becomes who's available, and this is equally true for location and studio work. There is very little opportunity to do a deal. Instead of taking time to pick carefully a group of less famous and less expensive technicians and artists, the safest decision may be to go for the most expensive.

Furthermore, it is extremely important that plans and bookings can be made firmly. If an agency cannot commit itself, everything and everyone has to be pencilled-in; and if the client does not confirm in good time the agency often loses technicians and artists, resulting in the shoot having to be postponed and extra money spent as a result. To get the most economical production, ensure that plenty of time is allowed to plan the production programme; and, equally importantly, that there is plenty of time after production to ensure that the best possible end-result is obtained from the production material.

This timetable cannot be generalized – but it must be *agreed* for each and every occasion; and properly recorded.

Appointing and involving production companies early

A key factor in achieving essential financial and timing control procedures is a complete involvement of producers and suppliers very early in the process. This applies equally in principle to all media.

It is essential for TV to appoint the director and production company as early as possible, so that the director can get involved with the idea from the beginning.

Do not indulge in competitive quotes for the sake of it. If the production company required gives a quote that is within budget, and with a breakdown which shows that its costs and mark-up are reasonable, then go with it. This will obtain maximum involvement from the production company and the director.

Some advertisers feel that by getting competitive quotes they are keeping a check on costs. But competitive quotes should only be asked for when genuinely two (or more) production companies, who are equally suited to the job, are quoting competitively. They should not be used just as a check on someone else's quote. The reason is normally transparent and the results unrealistic. These quotes can also be misleading when asked for in a hurry, because they will tend to be padded to allow for all the 'uncertainties'.

Nevertheless, it is only reasonable for the advertiser to be reassured that a quote is both competitive and soundly based. Leo Burnett has a system of costing a commercial initially *before* it goes to the production company for a formal quotation. This helps the producer in discussion with the production company, as he has a pretty good idea of what the commercial should cost. It enables the agency to explain the quote in detail, including director and crew rates and production company mark-up.

The pre-production meeting

Although this critical meeting is primarily considered in terms of TV, in practice this is (and should be) only a more formal version of discussions on production for other media. It is probably the one and only occasion when the writer, art director, producer and account director meet across the table with the film director and his producer, together with the advertiser.

The agency producer chairs the meeting. Its purpose is to examine and discuss the production in all its aspects. The agenda consists of the director's interpretation of the script, how he will shoot the commercial, photographs of the intended location, casting recommendations etc.

It is essential that all parties emerge from the meeting completely satisfied with the shooting plan, and that a complete record is made both of the firm decisions and options to be explored.

Additional press and print considerations

Print production has some major differences from television production, primarily in that there is a change in supplier half way through the production process. In television or cinema the production company is responsible for turning the script into film and for providing the final prints that go on-air. In the press, the original illustration, be it a photograph or a drawing, is produced by one supplier − the photographer or the artist − and is then passed on to *different* suppliers who provide the typesetting and the block-making or final artwork which is required by the paper or magazine. However, the principles of cost control apply equally here as in TV.

It is important to remember that photography and artwork can take as long to produce as film − sometimes longer. Also, copy dates on many colour publications can be up to two or three months. So a timing plan on colour press needs to be ideally just as generous as one on TV, if you do not want to incur high overtime costs.

Although there are many more suppliers for print, it is still important to involve these as early as possible in order to explore new opportunities and identify potential problems. This is equally true for those involved in the reproduction stages as well as the initial preparation and photographic sessions.

Because of the great variety in reproduction standards in print, the choice of suppliers to fit the media is critical. There is no point in having the most expensive retoucher and the most expensive platemaker, if the product and the media being used are not going to benefit from this high-priced talent.

Post-production budget reconciliation

It is unlikely that the pre-production estimate coincides exactly with the actual costs incurred, so it is sensible to have a post-production reconciliation meeting when the agency and production company explain how the actual costs compared with those budgeted. Usually overspends and underspends cancel each other out. But if there are real savings, than a credit should be requested.

6

Placing advertising effectively

So far we have concentrated solely on the advertisements. Our environment has been professional and data-orientated. Our target does not see it that way: to them advertisements are just a small part of the media they use for relaxation and information. We have to understand their point of view, to set advertisements in their overall media context.

It is the agency's job to recommend, agree and buy the space and time in which the advertisements appear. To do this effectively we have both to understand media and to be aware of the brand's marketing strategy. Putting the two together is the job of the media planner. Executing the plan is the job of the media buyer.

This is not a textbook covering in detail the media research we have to analyse, the history of the media themselves or the complexities of ratecards. It does not forecast media changes to come in the 1980s or comment on current controversies, or go deeply into some fundamental issues such as budget-setting. All these have been covered elsewhere.* What this chapter does cover is the agency point of view on media as part of campaign planning.

The object here is to provide the reader with insight into the judgements we make when building and carrying out media recommendations.

The media man has to ensure that the advertising so carefully created will most effectively sell to the people we require to reach. This can be expressed in another way: the media department's objective is to develop media plans to reach the *right people* in the *right context* at the *right price*.

*In particular *Spending Advertising Money* has been revised for its fourth edition by Simon Broadbent and Brian Jacobs, published by Business Books in 1984. The Burnett Media Department contributes monthly to *Media World* current media data and comment.

Data

In performing this function no media person can rely only on seat-of-the-pants judgements. He needs to identify what data will aid him in achieving the right end result. There are six categories of data that we most commonly use — these will now be considered in turn.

Media audience data

This tells us who consumes the media available; who watches television or listens to the radio; who reads which newspaper and what magazine. These data are generally provided by Joint Industry Committees. Their quality and detail vary considerably, as do their frequency of issue and sample sizes; thus their validity and usefulness also vary.

Investigation of these data helps to identify which media and parts thereof are most appropriate for reaching a specific target audience. The more refinements we make to the target audience definition, the more relevant analysis of the data becomes.

Product-media data

These provide a greater understanding of the people who consume different types of products and services.

It aids the identification of the media target audience and helps define target weights, that is the relative importance of the different segments that comprise the broad target audience.

The Target Group Index (TGI) is often used by us as a data source. We can obtain on our own computer terminal cross-tabulations between product use and media use. We are able to use the profile and weight of usership of any particular product to evaluate the relative efficiency of different media for reaching these people.

The reliability of these data will vary according to the overall market size and individual product penetration. The product data alone often provide useful guidance in the early discussions to decide on the target audience.

Media cost data

Obviously data on the cost of the media are important in

deciding which medium or combination to recommend, though not as important as its sales effectiveness.

The media provide details of the cost per advertisement in their ratecards. Nowadays these tend to be complex and flexible, so offering the informed agency an opportunity to buy at a wide variety of rates, dependent on our requirements and on current market demand.

However, we do not actually buy time and space — we buy audiences. Ultimately, we buy sales. The ability to judge between media audiences demands some form of audience data to which costs per advertisement can be applied. Only then will cost comparisons be meaningful. Moreover, it is not a media decision alone as to the choice and combination of media to be used. The factual input has also to be tempered with judgements about communication and sales-effectiveness.

Sales data

Sales data are extremely important to the media department. The manufacturer is, of course, the usual source of these data and we encourage him to provide the maximum information. The data will often include ex-factory shipments, values and profitability, as well as retail and consumer audit statistics. The media planner uses the data to allocate the budget, to allow for the seasonal and geographical variation in media costs.

Advertising expenditure data

It is important to know what the competition is up to and where the advertiser stands in his share of the advertising voice. This enables the media plan to be written with the knowledge of previous competitive practice, and with an allowance for possible future spending.

Study of competitors' activity can also uncover an area of weakness in the media strategy which we can exploit; examples are a television area undersupported relative to brand share, and periods of the year when a higher share of voice could be achieved with a lower investment.

In some markets the ability to maximize the value of advertising may depend on exploiting gaps in competitive campaigns. This is particularly true for motor cars, and an example of the influence of the market environment on budget size and media deployment is contained in the last chapter on the launch of the Metro.

Campaign effectiveness — tracking study data

In Chapter 8 we explain how consumer reactions to our advertising are studied. The most common response analysed is sales, from shop audit or diary panel data. However, it is in tracking studies, where we examine consumer response information in relation to advertising expenditure, that we get our clearest picture of the effect of our advertising. A key issue for planning any campaign is to maximize the length of time over which the advertising is working.

The decay of people's memories is caused by competitive activity as well as by normal forgetting: we operate usually in very crowded markets. We always aim to achieve a high and more-or-less permanent **base** of people who can remember our brand having been advertised, or who are able to recall what we said. But whether this is high or low, it is important to know how quickly awareness falls to that level.

Often the **half-life** of advertising can be well determined — that is, how long after our advertisement appeared when recall or awareness has had half its overall result. We have therefore been able to construct, and offer to our planners and buyers on their computer terminals, a model called **BAT** (Budget Allocation over Time). This takes a given budget and half-life and shows how response will vary over the year for different time plans. Our pattern of advertising over time can therefore be organized to maximum effect. Examples of how tracking study data have been used for specific brands are contained in the case histories on Cadbury's Flake, Kellogg's Super Noodles, Body Mist and Metro.

A decade ago, it was common to have an annual media plan. The allocation across the year was made well in advance of the advertisements appearing so good media value could be obtained this way. Fierce pre-emptive buying on television now means that later buyers can disrupt our own careful plan, and we have to keep on our toes up to the last minute. Advertisers have got into the habit of committing money later and later. Thus media buying — and even planning — runs to a shorter timetable.

The practical timing for media decisions is nowadays less critical than for the production timetable, which has been discussed above. If the advertiser commits his media money at the same time as we are producing the actual advertisement, our media department usually has enough time to plan and negotiate.

We begin by identifying the main task as a logical extension of the manufacturer's marketing strategy and our overall campaign objectives.

Effective media planning must certainly consider all the options, some on which experience is extremely limited, and some for which performance data are at best very general. The planning role is a delicate balancing of the familiar and relatively certain, with exciting forays into the unknown.

Obviously a product launch or relaunch will require a media solution different from that for an ongoing campaign. A change in creative execution in a previously used medium may well require additional weight to establish early awareness. A product with a regular purchase frequency will require a pattern of media different from one infrequently purchased. And so on.

Both our analysis of past brand performance and our general agency experience provide valuable guidance in deciding on the right plan to reach the right people.

Knowing who it is that we should be talking to is all-important. Great care must be taken in describing the target audience. This can be done in the following two ways, in addition to using the data already described.

Who are the target audience?

We can use demographics (for example, age and social class), the traditional way of describing target audiences. We can use Leo Burnett Life Style research to identify the target in a different way — by their feelings and beliefs. This has been a particularly valuable media planning tool in our own work on the Austin Rover account, especially for new product launches.

From this data source we are able to build a 'word picture' of the likely characteristics and type of person who will form the core of our target group. In conjunction with other qualitative data it can often provide a very valuable input and background for the media planners before they move into the use of quantitative analyses. Its role has been as a contributing factor to the direction in emphasis of schedule construction, rather than to act as a discriminator between titles.

We found the TGI itself to be of value on our Scottish and Newcastle breweries business where, with certain filters, we were able to identify when heavy drinkers viewed television, who they were and whether there were any differences in viewing patterns between those who were 'take home' and 'in-pub' consumers. This extensive piece of work enabled us to refine our approach to television buying against our target group, and not only indicated the type of time and programme which should be bought, but also what should be avoided!

Where is the target audience?

The target definition should identify the regional requirements of the media plan. We can then look at **ACORN** – a classification of residential neighbourhoods – and identify those types of neighbourhoods that are most likely to consume a particular type of product. For example, ACORN enabled us in the development of our poster buying brief for Perrier to identify quite precisely which areas were likely to be of greatest value. It allowed our outdoor buying unit to confine their negotiations with the poster contractors to very precise geographical areas and, ultimately, sites within those neigh-bourhoods. All of these data are available through the TGI once a product use definition has been agreed.

As media costs continue to increase at a faster rate than marketing funds, there is a growing move towards more regional marketing and advertising, towards concentration on key geographical groups.

Ultimately, we must know what type of person we are looking to reach and with what media we can best reach them.

Media objectives

The next stage is to establish the media objectives, the media tasks. Obviously any objectives begin with the need to reach the target audience, but this has to be refined. How many of them do we want to reach, and how often?

It could be physically impossible or totally impractical and unaffordable to reach everybody. A lesson here may well be that limiting coverage could yield a more effective campaign, communicating to fewer people but for a longer period.

How often do we want to reach them? There is so much received wisdom about the optimum level of frequency that some find it difficult to accept that advertising works in different markets at different levels of frequency. It is also important here to take account of competitive weight.

It must be remembered that definitions and calculations vary by media. It is worth while establishing what 80 per cent cover, for example, really means. Will it differ by television area? Does 80 per cent adult cover mean 70 per cent men and 90 per cent women? Such differences could be very important.

Individual media are measured differently. Research techniques, sample sizes, questionnaires, analyses available, the frequency of data collection − all of these vary. The Leo Burnett media research unit was established with the express intention of sifting through the masses of different data and surveys available. We have to guide our media planners towards that which is acceptable and usable and away from unreliable data.

In many cases appropriate information is just not available, and one of our major aims has been to encourage the collection and presentation of new data more precisely geared to media planning questions and decisions.

In addition, the manufacturer's marketing objectives may ask for emphasis on particular selling or promotional cycles where significant trade and sales force activity is planned. These requirements should also be referred to in the media objectives and any specific influence required on the trade should be highlighted.

Finally, there may be a requirement for testing either a different weight or mix of activity or an alternative creative execution. Any such test demands its own unique set of objectives and strategy. These should be the subject of a secondary proposal separate from the main media recommendation.

Media strategy

Our overall media strategy will indicate how the objectives will be achieved. In many cases the main inter-media decisions will have been taken as part of earlier campaign discussions involving the advertiser and creatives. Nevertheless, there is still much to be resolved which will involve considerable judgement in arriving at the best balance of media, and the way in which individual media are to be used.

The experienced media planner will have a very close understanding of the role each medium could play in achieving the objectives. He has a detailed knowledge of the various strengths and weaknesses of the media and will refer to these when presenting the case for the media selected.

Once the main inter-media decision has been made, the media planner is faced with a number of detailed alternatives, each of which need attention, discussion and a conclusion or recommendation for a course of action. It is at this stage that the media planner will involve the agency's specialist buyers for an accurate understanding of the media market that will prevail in the advertising period under discussion. The role of specialist buyers within agency media departments is growing with the ever-increasing fragmentation of media.

For example, the Leo Burnett local media unit was established with the express intention of developing a very close understanding of outdoor, cinema, radio and local press – all are media that can be bought from a town outwards.

Figures 6.1 and 6.2 outline the detailed decisions of timing, location and advertisement weight. Figure 6.1 summarizes the considerations and steps in non-press inter-media planning, and Figure 6.2 identifies the steps involved in press planning.

Obviously each media plan is uniquely created to meet the specific requirements of each product. There is no standard media plan, just as there is no standard creative solution.

Placing the advertising

The objectives have been set, the plan has been established, the media have been chosen, the budget has been identified. It is now the job of the media buyer to place advertising within the required medium to the best possible effect.

CONSIDERATIONS   **STEPS**

Budget
Cost of advertising Desired weight of advertising Total market sales Product sales

Seasonal sales profiles/opportunities → DISTRIBUTION OF BUDGET OVER TIME
Variations in seasonal media costs

Distribution of product → SELECTION OF AREAS
Media weight or market tests
Competitive advertising

Demographic profile of region → WEIGHT OF ADVERTISING BY AREA

Retail structure of region

Size and extent of region

Figure 6.1 Non-press inter-media planning (television, radio, outdoor, cinema)

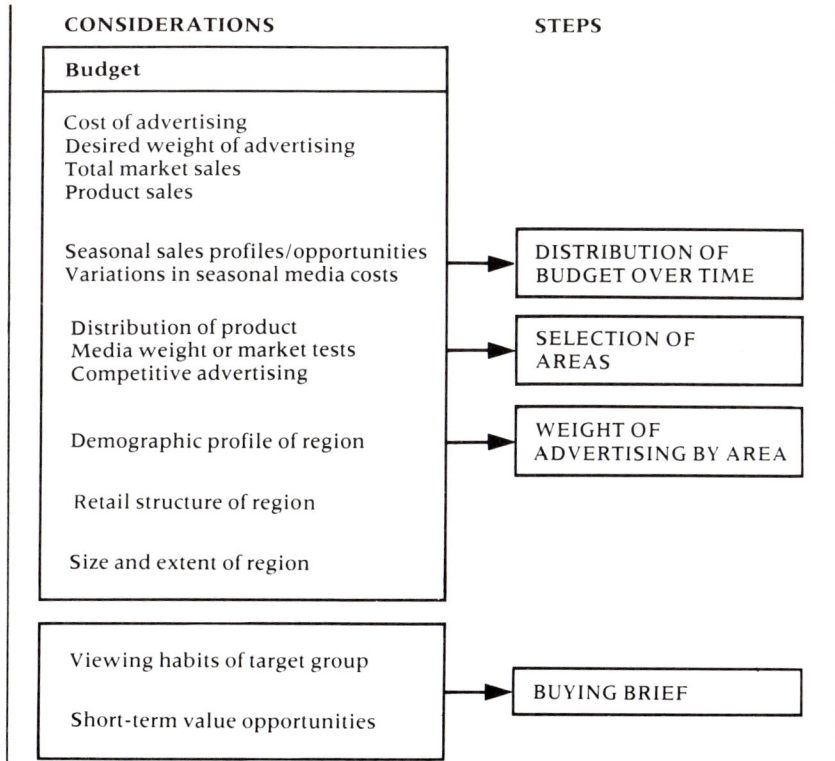

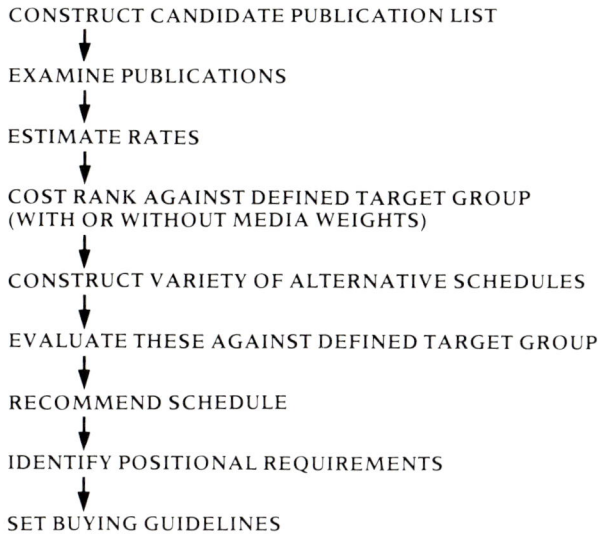

Viewing habits of target group → BUYING BRIEF

Short-term value opportunities

CONSTRUCT CANDIDATE PUBLICATION LIST
↓
EXAMINE PUBLICATIONS
↓
ESTIMATE RATES
↓
COST RANK AGAINST DEFINED TARGET GROUP
(WITH OR WITHOUT MEDIA WEIGHTS)
↓
CONSTRUCT VARIETY OF ALTERNATIVE SCHEDULES
↓
EVALUATE THESE AGAINST DEFINED TARGET GROUP
↓
RECOMMEND SCHEDULE
↓
IDENTIFY POSITIONAL REQUIREMENTS
↓
SET BUYING GUIDELINES

Figure 6.2 Steps involved in press intra-media planning

Media buying is not just about achieving the cheapest cost 'per thousand'. Rather, it is about placing advertising within a media context that will ensure that the advertisement has the best opportunity to communicate, and then negotiating the best terms.

In press, this can be described as obtaining the best balance of position against cost. In particularly crowded media, buying a premium position can be much more advantageous than simply aiming for the cheapest price.

In television, buying spots that contribute significantly to cover can be more beneficial than simply buying the highest total ratings.

Accountability

Finally, we must be accountable to the advertiser for what we have done. We must evaluate our performance and describe to the advertiser how well we have spent his money.

Sophisticated systems unique to Leo Burnett ensure that we suggest relevant assessments — particularly monitoring our coverage and frequency performance relative to the set objectives.

Media planning and buying is a dynamic, ongoing process in an ever-changing environment. This demands regular assessments of what is being achieved. These reappraisals are also a learning process that enables us continually to improve our planning and to find better ways next time of achieving our objectives.

7

Multinational advertising: agony or ecstasy?

Most of this book deals with the situation where we are working on a brand for a single client, who usually speaks with one voice at all levels of the organization. It can be more complicated when the manufacturer is a multinational company approaching the development of advertising on a regional or global basis. There is then not only a local office — say in London — but also a headquarters — say in the United States — to work with. Or, of course, there may be a British headquarters and local offices serviced by our agencies on the Continent, in the Middle East or elsewhere.

The steps of developing a strategy and creative work now take on another dimension. Making effective advertising under these conditions becomes an involved and complicated process, requiring sometimes the skill of a United Nations negotiator and the patience of Job — plus, of course, all the normal skills and disciplines for developing good domestic advertising.

The past ten years have seen an accelerating trend for multinational manufacturers to approach their marketing and advertising programmes globally. These companies have had to rethink their whole structure and organization to cope with this changed approach. At the same time, it has placed a heavy burden on their advertising agencies. Often, if the advertiser himself is not properly organized, it is on the agency that the responsibility falls to agree, implement and police the campaign. For an internationally appointed agency network, working with the client in every market, this responsibility can lead to friction with the client's local manager who has previously been used to much greater autonomy. For a manufacturer who attempts to advertise globally with different (usually domestic) agencies in each country, the problems are almost always greater still, for then the whole responsibility for coordination falls back on him — and few companies have the staff, control or expertise to carry this out.

Yet, those companies and agencies which have learnt to operate successfully in this way have found that international coordination can be highly rewarding. Our experience of both success and failure with different organizational structures can therefore help those treading this particular tightrope. The secret of success is not as hard to find as is sometimes imagined by those who try and fail. Very often, the real cause for failure is a lack of understanding of what exactly they are trying to do and why they are trying to do it. Joining a bandwagon just for the sake of it is no good at all — first, you've got to know where it's going. And then you need the will to see the journey out to the end, even though the early parts of the road may be rough and bumpy.

Why centralize?

Why should companies who have traditionally, and very often successfully, operated on an international policy of allowing local autonomy in marketing and advertising decisions decide that it will be better to adopt the same approach everywhere? Is it just to make the showreel at headquarters look more consistent, or are there sound business reasons that make it good sense?

There are probably two key factors which have contributed more than any other. First, there is the realization that good ideas are hard to find, and a good idea that has worked in one place at one time will very often work elsewhere, if dressed up and presented in the right way. Second, there is a growing understanding that people, cultures and habits are not really as different as local managers would often have their head office believe. Particularly with functional brands where the product itself and the target market — indeed the competition — vary little market by market, there is no need to re-invent the wheel every time.

Other benefits are often quoted as reasons for a global approach: the direct savings in advertising production costs that allow more of the budget to be put into the media; the savings in local management time that permit greater effort to be put against other key marketing issues and local problems; the development of a single unified image for a brand at a time when consumers are travelling internationally themselves to an ever greater extent; the growth of international print media and satellite television starting to become reality.

Manufacturers should recognize that these benefits are nothing more than positive spin-offs, by-products from following a global approach. They do not represent, by themselves, reasons strong enough to abandon local marketing. The only reasonable criterion must be whether a global approach will sell more merchandise, more profitably, in total than the sum of different individual local approaches. If not, the exercise is better not begun.

Agency implications

What are the implications of this trend to global marketing for our own structure?

First, it means a need to have strong offices in all the major advertising markets. Major multinational manufacturers expect and deserve the same level of service and sophistication in the overseas markets that they are used to in the home territory. Also, as advertisers look more and more to appoint networks rather than separate agencies country by country, the 'weakest link in the chain' becomes highly relevant – being impressive in a few countries is no longer enough.

Second, it means we have to invest in experienced coordination staff, and to set up the necessary systems and backup. Very often, particularly in the early stages of a client moving to global advertising, the major part of the coordination burden falls on these agency people as the client tries to develop his own system from scratch.

Third, it means a need to find and develop internationally minded people in the local markets, and to train those previously involved only on domestic business to think with an international outlook. There is no doubt that for both client service and creatives, the international rules are different, and the players must accept this from the outset and be prepared and happy to operate within the international rules. There is nothing worse than one person trying to play rugby when everybody else thinks that the game is soccer. In these circumstances it is far better for the odd man out to leave the pitch and seek pastures new, otherwise the whole game can be jeopardized for everybody else.

Another hurdle for advertising

The phrase 'one-sight, one-sound' has become very fashionable amongst companies embarking on a multinational advertising venture for the first time. It has been taken up as a rallying call, an expression of what they think they are trying to do. Unfortunately, few who use the phrase have stopped to ask themselves what it really means, or how such a philosophy is best implemented in practice.

Too many firms think that to reach the holy grail of 'one-sight, one-sound' all you have to do is run the same commercials everywhere. 'One-sight, one-sound' is translated into 'one piece of celluloid' — but this is neither intelligent nor sensible.

The phrase 'one-sight, one-sound' should be a statement of intent. It sets out the aim of giving the brand the same look, the same feel, the same personality wherever it is sold and advertised; the same tone, the same positioning, the same advertising strategy — but not necessarily exactly the same advertising execution.

Sometimes the same execution will work equally effectively in every country, but this is the exception. Normally a good strategy and a strong advertising idea can best be capitalized on by intelligent use of local as well as international executional input.

For example, the Marlboro Cowboy campaign, devised by Leo Burnett in Chicago in 1955, is probably the most successful international advertising campaign there has ever been. It transformed Marlboro from a small-share US brand, primarily smoked by women, into what is today the world's best-selling cigarette. In every country the Marlboro Cowboy campaign has been an unqualified success, building volume and brand share year by year.

The way the campaign has been implemented country by country is an excellent example of an intelligent interpretation

The Marlboro Cowboy
in Nigeria

The US Marlboro Cowboy
as he has ridden across
Europe

of 'one-sight, one-sound'. The strategy is the same in every country, the advertising idea is the same in every country, but the executions are not. In Nigeria, for example, the cowboy is black; in Australia he is an Australian cowboy in the outback; in Hong Kong he is not a cowboy at all but a ranch owner, recognizing the oriental desire to associate with success and material possessions. Everywhere the integrity of the campaign is preserved, and everywhere its full potential is realized by tailoring the execution to the local market.

Organization

How do we and our international clients organize ourselves to operate a global marketing and advertising policy? Perhaps the best way to illustrate the variety of possible approaches is to describe the two poles of the spectrum.

At one extreme is a system of *centralization*. In such a system all major strategy and executional work takes place at the centre between the client's headquarters and ours. The agency 'headquarters' can be either a small central staff whose purpose is to operate and coordinate such international business; or, more usually, the local office in the country where the client headquarters is situated — the 'lead' agency concept. The centre, for both client and agency, has line responsibility and the role of the offices in the local markets is to implement the centrally agreed programmes. This means working on translations or any other adaptions to the creative work that may be necessary, planning and buying the media, carrying out research, tactical and promotional activity, and, of course, inputting as much as possible, or allowed, into the decisions of the centre.

Such a system, thus described, sounds authoritarian; and, if implemented insensitively or dogmatically, it can be just that. However, for certain companies and products it can make a lot of sense to operate this way: if the product is the same and is packaged the same in each country; if it is used in the same way everywhere and for the same purpose; if the profile of the consumer is broadly the same, as well as the consumer's desires and aspirations; and above all, if a certain strategy and advertising idea has already been proved successful in one or more markets and checked out in the others − then such a system of centralization may well be the best way of maximizing global sales and profits.

At the other extreme is a system of pure *coordination*. This is where the advertiser's local office still retains a high degree of autonomy in marketing and advertising matters. The agency then works with him at the local level in a normal or domestic client/agency relationship. The coordination service provided by the centre is designed to supply global knowledge and resources in order to assist the marketing effort in the individual countries. It also usually assumes a degree of quality control.

Clearly, between these two extremes there are many other permutations possible. The key variables in each case are the degrees of flexibility allowed at the local level. At the end of the day, whatever system is used, the objective remains exactly the same − to optimize company and agency resources in order to produce more effective advertising in every country.

Our choice of operating procedure depends largely on how the client is organized. We can, and do, line up against both extremes − pure centralization and pure coordination − as well as in many ways in between. But it is no good for us to try to centralize if the client operates a more flexible system, or vice versa; this is the quickest way to cause problems and friction at a local level. We must, on our side, match as closely as possible the structure and systems the client himself is operating. We can, of course, advise him, from our own experience, whether his current or planned organization is likely to work effectively. We can lead him towards the method most likely to work for his kind of product.

Examples

Our largest client worldwide, Philip Morris, has a well-defined system that enables all involved, whether client or agency, to understand clearly what is decided at the centre and what can be carried out locally. Essentially, it is a system of centralization for strategy development and coordination for campaign executions and tactical activities. The advertising strategies for the major international brands are laid down by the centre and cannot be altered in any country.

However, countries are responsible for developing their own campaign executions, within certain well-defined guidelines. These executions then have to be approved by the centre before they can be run. The local markets remain responsible for their own media planning and buying, for their own research, for production and other tactical activities.

Memorex, on the other hand, currently adopts a much more centralized procedure. Here, both strategy and executional development are the responsibility of the centre. The local markets input to development, but the final decision rests firmly with the centre. Once the campaign has been finalized, the local client and agency's role is to adapt it for the local market.

The question then arises, of course, how much local adaptation is possible or allowable? Certain elements have to be changed for the advertisements to make any sense — translation into the local language, for example. Also, there may be changes forced by local legal considerations or censorship bodies. Thereafter, it becomes much more difficult to draw the line between justifiable change to improve local effectiveness, and change for change's sake.

On some international accounts we ourselves, in London, are the centre, and are responsible for developing the advertising that will run in many countries.

For the Seven-Up Company, for example, we develop in London television and cinema advertising that runs in over fifty countries. In most of these countries, local budgets are simply not large enough to fund significant adaptations, recuts or edits, even if they were desired. The usual limit of local change is language.

Therefore, we have to do our homework very thoroughly prior to developing the advertising. We have to go through many stages of discussion and liaison with the local markets to ensure that what we eventually produce will not only be acceptable, but highly effective, in the individual countries. The danger, of course, is to end up with advertising that is bland, that represents the lowest common denominator between all these countries − advertising that offends nobody. This must be resisted firmly; whilst everybody's opinions and desires can be listened to, it is impossible for all to be taken account of in the final executions, for often they are contradictory. The answer is to produce a sufficient range of executions so that there will be, amongst the pool, something that every country will find effective. In other words, do not aim for every execution to work in every country; that is just not feasible.

On the Cathay Pacific Airways account, we in London are not the centre, but one of the local offices. The centre in this case is Hong Kong, the home port of Cathay. Overall campaign strategy and theme is worked out between Cathay Pacific head office and Leo Burnett Hong Kong. Our role in London is to adapt the centrally produced creative work for UK use, and to make sure that any tactical advertising that we produce for local use only is consistent with the overall campaign strategy and theme.

In practice our role is greater than this; for, as the most important of all the out-ports, our views and input on the worldwide campaign must be heard and taken account of if that campaign is to be truly effective worldwide. Therefore a whole series of discussions and meetings take place between ourselves and our office in Hong Kong before any creative recommendation is placed before Cathay Pacific in Hong Kong. We, in turn, have made sure that our local client here in London is fully in the picture on how things are developing and has his own chance for input at an early stage. In this way, when the final recommendation is made there are no surprises, and everyone who will eventually run the campaign has made a contribution to its development. Even if all the comments do not have an effect in the end, at least they have been fully and frankly debated and considered. To be properly considered but rejected for sound reasons is acceptable; to be rejected without proper consideration is not.

Conclusions

The task facing those who have to create international advertising is a daunting one. Not only do all those skills and techniques outlined in other chapters of this book have to be brought to bear; but this has to be done against a more complex backcloth.

More considerations have to be taken into account, more opinions listened to, and more stages of approval successfully negotiated.

One guiding principle above all others can contribute to the development of a successful international campaign. This is to have a clear organization and allocation of responsibilities. Effective advertising does not just happen, it has to be managed. Management has to be unambiguous as well as determined.

8

Is our advertising effective?

If only we could be absolutely sure, at the time we put our advertising into production, that it was going to be sales effective!

Some research techniques have offered the assurance that they can tell good from bad at this stage. We get guidance from these techniques, but we do not trust them on this ultimate question.

Many advertising people believe they instinctively know good from bad. This ability is a major part of the job. We hope to have a good share of those who usually do know. But we do not pretend we are infallible. So as well as making our judgements as unbiased and as predictive as we can, we need some evaluation, after our campaign, of whether our advertising was effective. And in this way we improve our campaign as it goes on.

This chapter concentrates on one particular technique we use — statistical analysis of national sales and tracking study data.

This is because the results are exciting — we can often detect advertising effects more clearly than used to be thought possible. The findings can also be used directly as aids to decision-making. The advertiser can be helped to set his advertising budget, for example. Since we have to evaluate other factors affecting sales — of which price is usually the most important — we can also give him guidance on product pricing.

Numerical modelling is not, of course, the only method used in the agency. One of the most important precepts in campaign evaluation is to ensure that *all* available data are used. This includes much which cannot be quantified but is nonetheless valuable. We are trying to understand a single process: what happens when our consumers see our advertising. Each of the data sources we use is describing one aspect of this whole. Each of them is to some extent biased or imprecise or unrepresentative. We have to make the most honest assessment we can, which means combining all the evidence.

The planners at Leo Burnett spend most of their time in post-campaign evaluation, using other tools. They plan and assess area tests, they run analyses against media exposure. They get the feel for how consumers are changing from qualitative work, they use surveys which cover many relevant awareness, attitude and image dimensions.

All these help us to explain *how* the advertising is working. The agency is guided as to how we can improve our work. Is the strategy confirmed but the fine-tuning of the advertisements can be improved? Or in what way should the strategy be rewritten?

Before starting to think of improvement, we have to decide whether the current advertising is effective. Without this information we might wrongly change advertising too early – or we might continue to run poor advertising.

Measures to evaluate advertising

We now concentrate on two important measures by which advertising is judged:

■ consumer sales (as measured by Nielsen or other audits, or by regular consumer surveys such as **PPI**)

■ awareness (as measured in tracking studies, often brand saliency or proven recall of advertising).

These are measures which our advertisers use: the bottom line is what advertising is for, and tracking studies are bought by them to see how consumers react to advertising. It is, therefore, a priority for us to explain movements in sales or awareness and to understand how advertising causes these movements.

In this way Leo Burnett forces itself to be accountable to the advertiser for the real value of its work. Our responsibility does not end when the advertiser agrees to run our recommendation. It ends only when we jointly agree what experience has taught us – whether or not he got value for money, and how we can do better next time.

In analysing sales it is nearly always necessary to bring in other factors, which often have a larger effect than does the advertising. This is not to minimize advertising's contribution. Beecham area tests, carefully analysed, have shown sales changes of 20 per cent and more, due solely to advertising. One such analysis is reported in the Flake case history.

Product quality, price relative to those of competitors, and distribution are always considered. For example, in preparing the Sunday Express strategy we used our analysis of the effect of cover price on its circulation. Special factors such as in-store activity, seasonality, weather, competitors' actions, and so on, may also be relevant. Tracking study measures, on the other hand, are nearly always pure advertising effects: the weight of advertising and its quality explain nearly all. The Body Mist example shows a very clear effect of advertising on tracking study scores. Cadbury analyses are our largest body of evidence on this point, and we also see it clearly with Austin Rover research. In-store work which precedes the campaign sometimes means that awareness of the brand, or even claimed advertisement recall, start to rise before we are actually on-air.

Post-campaign might seem to be too late to be worrying about the advertising. After all, production costs have already been incurred and much of the media money has been committed. But actually it is the best time, in the sense that we are now in the real world, subject to all the noise of competitors' advertising; our consumers are making real decisions to buy or not to buy, using advertising as one input in that decision. The hothouse of advertising development cannot help but be artificial: 'It is not possible to measure sales effectiveness in a laboratory', wrote Alan Hedges. We believe it is also impossible to measure accurately advertising visibility or its efficiency in branding.

Approach to numerical evaluation

There are two key ideas in measuring numerically the effectiveness of advertising. The first is that advertising does not work all at once and then disappear — we need a way of handling the decay of its effects over weeks or months. The second is that, once we have made proper allowance for time, we can usually apply normal **regression** methods to estimate how large the effects are. We need not assume that each advertisement, still less each campaign, has equal effect; we can look for differences from an overall fit, or fit different parts separately. We can also allow for other factors simply by using multiple regression. The problems with this technique are discussed in textbooks: the main one we meet is that two so-called independent factors sometimes actually move together – for example, the advertising burst coincides with an improvement in distribution, or a new campaign with a price change. It is then difficult or impossible to disentangle the factors.

Modelling marketing data is not a mechanical procedure aimed simply at getting the best fit: commonsense, other information and experience come into play. When we succeed in getting a fit, a model is suggested to our clients, it is not proven; its parameters are estimates, not facts. For example, the Super Noodles model, reported in detail in the case history with very illuminating results, is only one of two analyses available to Kelloggs.

To show how this can be done we take an example from Cadbury tracking study data – selected because the findings are clear and interesting, and because more detail and comment have been published by Cadbury so the example can be followed up by the reader.

We take three years' data from Cadbury's Dairy Milk; proven advertisement awareness is to be modelled. Two campaigns, on different strategies, ran over this time. The fit we used assumed six weeks' half-life in the decay of advertising's effects, a length estimated by looking at how awareness moved over a number of confectionery brands (the definition of 'half-life' is given below).

First we fit the period covered by campaign A: we find a 'base' of 19 per cent; i.e. awareness falls to about this level after a period without advertising. The reaction to adstock is an increase of seven awareness points for each 100 **TVR**s over four weeks. Both of these are relatively high figures. Figure 8.1 shows the raw data and the thirty-second equivalent TVRs which cause the awareness. The full line is the calculated fit, reproducing the main movement and many of the details of the data. Fits as good as this are not unusual in tracking study work.

Now consider the effects of changing to campaign B. We study this by assuming that it has equal efficiency (in creating

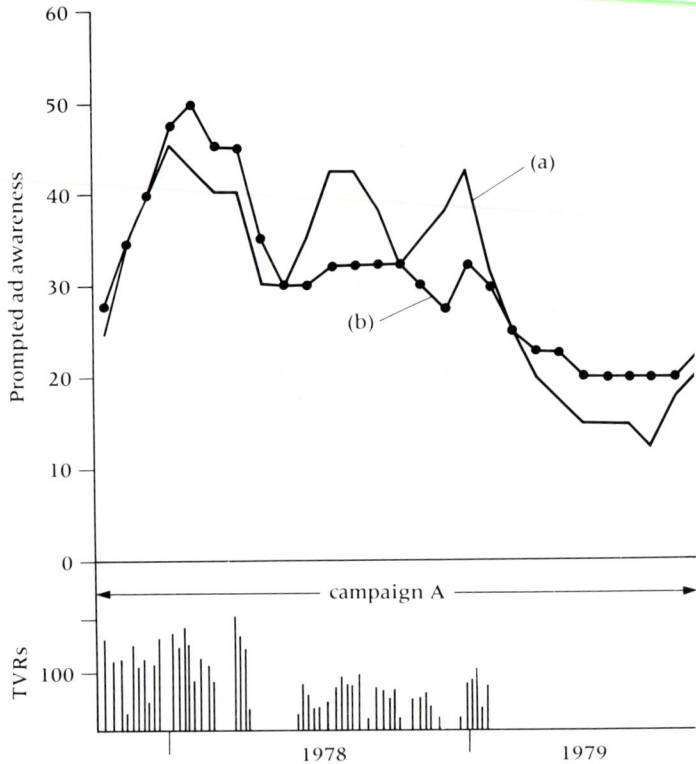

Figure 8.1 Cadbury's Dairy Milk — campaign A (a) actual (b) fitted

awareness) with campaign A, so we extend the same model to predict the new effects, using the appropriate TVRs, in Figure 8.2. The actual data are shown for campaign B. It clearly falls

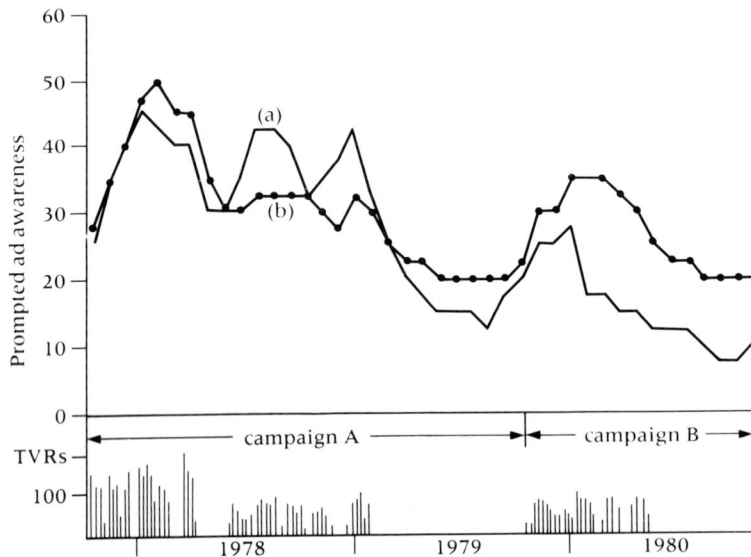

Figure 8.2 Cadbury's Dairy Milk — campaign B added (a) actual (b) fitted from campaign A

below the prediction. Campaign B got lower TVRs than campaign A, so we expect the results to be lower; but the actual is clearly worse than those expected, even after allowing for reduced weight.

We also carried out a separate fit over the period of campaign B. The results compare with campaign A as shown in Table 8.1. Clearly the reason why campaign B creates less awareness is that the 'base' resulting from campaign A has been eroded: by an abrupt change in the advertising we have lost 10 per cent of the target who felt they had seen Dairy Milk advertised recently. Subsequently campaign B was itself changed.

Campaign	Base	Slope (reaction to 100 TVRs)
A	19	7
B	9	6

Table 8.1

What have we gained by doing these fits? There are several important findings. We know the rate of decay over time at which awareness decreases – this helps us in scheduling. We know that the standard of creative work used in the second campaign is below that in the first (in creating awareness). In reaching this conclusion, we have allowed fully for the different advertising weights behind these campaigns. We also know that competitive advertising and other possible disturbing factors in fact had little effect on proven advertisement awareness for the brand.

The adstock model

Having shown by our example what we mean by modelling, we next give more detail on how we obtain such results. After that we give a second example, and we then describe other uses of the results and some conclusions.

There have been two main reasons for a breakthrough in the way marketing data can now be better understood: the **adstock** model and the microcomputer. The adstock model is based on a simple idea, used for decades by some statisticians in the analysis of time series. An action in one week, like one advertisement achieving 100 TVRs, has results which last many weeks. But its effect each week is a little lower than in the week before. We can think of our consumers' memories holding less and less of our copy point in mind, the amount kept (the retention factor) being, for example, 90 per cent of the preceding week's. Our 100 TVRs are in this way treated as spread over succeeding weeks. After a certain time (seven weeks at a retention factor of 90 per cent) it has had half its total effect − we call this the half-life of our advertising. Of course we do not normally have only 100 TVRs, but a whole schedule in preceding weeks. Each week's previous advertising contributes something to the effect in any particular following week: the cumulated, decayed effect is called *adstock*.

Now bring in the measure we wish to model − proven recall each week in the tracking study example given. By regressing recall on the adstock in the same week we generally get a good relationship. The regression has three parameters: the *base* previously referred to, the *slope* (the amount by which recall rises with adstock), and the **half-life.** These parameters are estimated during the fitting process.

To carry out such calculations we have in the past used time-sharing on a large outside computer − through the Comshare system − and we still do. But we also have other jobs to do. Most marketing companies spend a lot of money on collecting data. They study consumer sales. They put tracking studies into the field to look at consumers' awareness and images of brands, at their awareness and recall of advertising. There are also many government data and industry sources, such as BARB and MEAL, which companies acquire.

In our experience, these data are under-used. Most people have neither the experience nor the time to study the numbers properly or to unravel the relationships between the decisions they or their competitors took, and what happened to consumers' attitudes and behaviour. Too often all that is done is to compare this period's sales with the last period's, or with this period's last year.

There are many reasons for this neglect of an important opportunity. It is laborious to keep written records up to date and easily available. Calculating averages or plotting the data (often the best way to see what the trends are) is even more time-consuming. Deeper statistical analysis is beyond most people.

Of course, research companies do their best to provide useful summaries, but they cannot anticipate what will be most useful to each of their many clients. It is rarely economic for them to provide proper analyses, and certainly not when this requires several sources, which is usually the case.

Leo Burnett has set up a small analysis unit in the planning department. It has a staff of four – and an Apple IIe computer. This is cheaper than a time-sharing service, though we pay for this in time spent developing our own programs. The explosion in micro services (calling on the enthusiasm of many gifted amateurs as well as professionals) means that some programs are available relatively cheaply. Visicalc, plotting and statistical packages are obvious examples. To get such services on the mainframe would be much more expensive.

It has become much easier to write as well as to design programs. The simplicity of the BASIC language and the availability of a variety of programming aids means that it is sometimes quicker to program the solution than to design a system for someone else to code.

The outlines of one application will make it clear what data sources and what quantities of data are involved in an application of ADS, our Apple Data Store suite of programs.

In one recent analysis, we were interested in a market of seven main brands. Including the market total and 'all others', we had nine 'products' to consider. The Television Consumer Audit gave us national sales, both in weight and in sterling, from which the price paid per unit could be calculated.

We are interested in more than the actual price: we want to remove inflation to look at constant prices; the brand's price relative to the market average is also important. We want shares of market as well as actual sales.

Going back nearly three years meant using thirty-five periods of four weeks. For each of these we now have nine products and six numbers. We are already up to a couple of thousand pieces of data.

Next we have tracking study data, also in four-week periods. If we look at just three measures – for example, brand awareness, one key image dimension and proven advertising recall – we have another thousand numbers.

Even with only national TVRs to measure advertising we have another problem. Our BARB tape, analysed on the mainframe, tells us how many equivalent thirty-second rating points each product bought. We use weeks as the unit in our work since experience has shown us that this fineness of detail is essential. We also know we have to go back in time beyond the start of our sales or consumer data. Hence our raw advertising data is up to nearly two thousand numbers.

It is clear that before our real analysis can start we have several tasks. First, we have to input the original data. This is not too laborious given an efficient data entry program.

Next, there are conversions of the raw data to get shares, constant prices, and so on. We have a 'calculating' program to create the new columns required. Finally, we have a method to get adstock, hardly possible except with a computer.

At the end we have perhaps some ten thousand numbers. All of them are held in less than a quarter of a small magnetic disc, 5¼ inches in diameter. This quantity is far too large to re-enter for each application, so we need permanent storage. Therefore the use of each of our bought programs (statistical package, time-series analysis, graphing, etc.) cannot be separate, though this is how they are designed. We ourselves have had to write the links between our data store, our standard programs and our special programs, as no commercially available service offers this.

Data presentation

It is not much good holding such data unless we can summarize and present it, as well as manipulate it.

This is a separate task. We have programs to print tables, to circulate averages, ranges, etc., and to plot the data.

This stage is very important. There is no point in subsequent analysis unless the results can be quickly and convincingly shown to people who use them. Our work on Simplicity, for example, produced averages and plots as its clearest findings, and these were much more important than time series analysis. A word like 'elasticity' − let alone 'regression coefficient' or 't-test' − is not in the normal language of a marketing man. When he uses the word 'parameter' he usually distorts its meaning. But the implications of such arcane rituals can usually be deduced from graphical representations.

This was the method used, for example, in the Super Noodles case history. The use of ADS showed us that advertising was a major factor in consumer sales, that the half-life of our advertising was about five weeks, that one campaign was more sales-effective than another, that price, distribution and (in a separate analysis) seasonality all played a part. In the Body Mist example we were able to explain tracking study movements by this adstock model. For Lucozade we showed that one positioning was superior to another, having taken into account several other factors which affected sales. All these examples are in later chapters.

After such analysis, what aids to decisions are available? The methods we have used longest are called **BAR** (Budget Allocation over Regions) and BAT (Budget Allocation over Time). These run on our mainframe, because we need them to be available to all our planners and TV buyers. They can see, for example, on their screen the effects of different allocations or schedules, and can improve these schedules. They can answer questions like:

■ 'Would two bursts be better than continuous advertising? When should they be?'

■ 'Should we move advertising away from expensive time, even though that is when sales peak?'

■ 'What awareness do we expect to create with that schedule?'

To run BAT we need the advertising decay rate, which is what our earlier analyses using ADS can sometimes find.

The next method we use is called BPA (Budgeting Pricing and Advertising). A later extension of this is called PAW (Price, Advertising and Weight) which also allows for product weight changes. Its object is to start with a brand's budget and see whether it can be improved. The 'improvement' is a balance between sales volume (often a key objective) and profit. In passing, we note that economists often assume that profit is the only objective of the firm. In the long run this may be true; but looking only a year forward (which is how most brands are planned) it is certainly untrue. Most firms could improve one year's profit by raising the product price and cutting spending on advertising. Volume is also important, if the firm is to stay in business.

To see how BPA works we take an application which uses numbers typical of major, advertised brands. Such a brand sells 25 million packs a year at the manufacturer's average selling price of 60p, generating £15 million. Other details can be seen in its budget (Table 8.2).

Fixed costs	2,750
Variable costs (36p per pack)	9,000
Advertising	1,000
Profit	2,250
Revenue	**15,000**

Table 8.2
Typical brand's budget
(£000)

We also input our estimate (derived from an ADS analysis, for example) of its price and advertising elasticities. For a 'typical' brand we have data which suggest these are −1.3 and 0.2; i.e. these are the percentages by which sales volume changes for a 1 per cent change in price or in spending on advertising.

We know also that typical **breakeven elasticities** are −2.5 and 0.17. Because actual price elasticity is much smaller than breakeven, it clearly pays to put up the price − but this, of course, loses volume. Because actual advertising elasticity is a little larger than breakeven, it just pays to increase advertising − and, of course, it also improves volume.

The purpose of BPA is to allow exploration of alternative policies and to produce new, improved budgets. There are, of course, more results given by BPA than in the following simplified case.

For example, for our 'typical brand' we can predict the effect of changing the price by one penny either way − and of changing spending on advertising by £400,000 (Table 8.3). Clearly, to increase volume we should raise spending on advertising, and the increase is much larger at the lowered price.

However, what is the cost of doing this? BPA also predicts the effect on profit (Table 8.4). The drop in price is unprofitable, as was suggested above in the comparison of actual and breakeven elasticities. Raising the spending on advertising is not on its own a recipe for much change in profit, but in combination with price an acceptable combination has emerged.

Adspend (£000)	800	1,200
Price 61p	−1,600,000	+400,000
Price 59p	−600,000	+1,500,000

Table 8.3
Change in sales volume

Adspend (£000)		800	1,200
Price	61p	+50	+150
Price	59p	−200	−100

Table 8.4
Change in profit (£000)

Fixed costs	2,750
Variable costs	9,150
Advertising	1,200
Profit	2,400
Revenue	15,500

Table 8.5
Possible new budget for
the brand (£000)

If priority is given to volume, we should increase spending on advertising while leaving the price unaltered. If we want profit and are not so interested in a volume change, we might move to an alternative budget, which is based on a price rise to 61p and an increase in spending on advertising, and which also gives a volume increase of 1.5 per cent (Table 8.5).

Obviously, in individual cases many different sorts of conclusion emerge; but every time the main budget decisions are illuminated.

Use of the findings

Having outlined our methods we can turn to the kind of advice we give the team on the business and our clients. (Those who have benefited from analysis services include Austin Rover, Beecham, Bradford & Bingley, Cadbury, Chivers Hartley, Kellogg, Kimberley-Clark, Nestlé/Crosse and Blackwell, Philip Morris and Scottish & Newcastle.)

We ourselves understand better how our advertising works in the real world: we can take a more realistic view of our own creative work. We can improve some of the other decisions we have to make, such as allocation over time or over areas. We can advise our clients about the likely effects of decisions they make, such as pricing the product.

These are examples of recommendations made recently:

■ 'It wasn't better distribution that got the sales gain − it was the lower price.'

■ 'If you increase **adspend**, profit will . . . and volume sales will ....'

■ 'If you cut adspend, you'll reduce profit − this year.'

- 'The ad strategy started to wear out from ....'

- 'Spend behind Brand F – not Brand G.'

- 'Your sales forecast, given the marketing decisions, is too optimistic.'

- 'Allowing for adspend changes, awareness is not improving.'

Conclusions

In the marketplace, our advertising's saliency, memorability, decay and sales effectiveness are all being tested against the real competition. What we learn from analysing marketplace data improves the internal standards and judgement which we have to use most of the time. For the brands whose sales we can 'explain', we can make better recommendations for future action.

Part 2
Case histories

9

Flake: short- and long-term advertising effects

Marketplace

The confectionery market is one of the largest consumer markets in the UK. Its value in 1982 was around £2,000 million; only tobacco and alcoholic drinks achieve higher figures. As a category it is purchased by virtually everyone, with child consumption representing only about a third of the market. On average everyone in the UK eats about 8oz of confectionery per week, giving us one of the highest consumption levels in the world. This figure has been virtually static for many years; the success of any brand therefore has to be at the expense of its competitors. This has made the confectionery market one of the most strongly competitive in the UK. The three major manufacturers – Cadbury, Rowntree and Mars – are among the country's heaviest advertisers, with more than £65 million being spent by the three giants on television alone during 1982.

Confectionery is purchased on many occasions and to fulfil many roles, ranging from the elaborate gift to an inexpensive self-indulgence or a replacement for a missed meal. The consumer sees clear differences between brands bought as gifts, those bought for sharing with friends or family, and products which are purchased primarily for self consumption. This last category, products purchased for self consumption, represents the largest sector of the market and the consumer has certain clear favourites. The largest brand is the Mars Bar, with over £100 million in annual retail sales. Other major brands in the Mars stable include Milky Way, Topic and Bounty, while Cadbury's key contenders are Flake, Crunchie and Double Decker.

Despite the consumers' predilection for each of these bars, they do not buy one or another exclusively. In a market hallmarked by its range of products, the consumer enjoys variety by developing his or her own repertoire of brands. This includes not only certain key brands which feature regularly, but also a wider range of secondary favourites which enjoy a less frequent rate of purchase.

The purpose of advertising in this market is usually to sustain a position, or to endeavour to secure a more central position, in the purchasing repertoire.

Flake has long been one of Cadbury's most important properties; its sustained growth during the early 1970s firmly consolidated its place as their most important contender in this key market sector. This continued until 1977 when the whole sector went through a depressed year, declining by some 7 per cent in volume. Flake's sustained growth faltered, causing a volume loss of 15 per cent, significantly worse than the category performance.

Part of this was felt to stem from a weight decrease in 1976 that had served to reduce the value for money offered by the brand. But it did not explain the total loss.

It became evident that there was a need for a more fundamental and detailed study of the brand to determine why the previous growth pattern was not being kept up and what would have to be done differently if a return to real growth was to be achieved.

The basic appeal of the product has remained unchanged for many years. Product, pack and advertising combined to establish a strong individual personality for the brand which had resulted in an increasingly strong consumer franchise. The advertising itself, first conceived in the late fifties to coincide with the brand's promotion on television, had remained surprisingly constant in its structure and message. Designed to reflect the undeniably self-indulgent nature of the product, the advertising promised a taste so delicious that it would give you the sensation of having been transported to a world where everyday cares just do not exist. This escapist message appealed greatly to the heaviest buyers of Flake, women

Only the crumbliest, flakiest

chocolate tastes like chocolate

never tasted before.

A Flake girl in 1982
(Gypsy Caravan)

typically aged between twenty-five and forty-five who represent the core of the brand's franchise.

Detailed qualitative research showed no slackening of the product's appeal to this group, who continued to find all aspects of the marketing mix relevant and motivating – although their consumption at up to two or three times per week was already so high that it was unlikely that they would represent significant opportunities for further volume growth.

If the important heavy users were unlikely to provide the path to growth, then what other routes existed? The Leo Burnett agency and the Cadbury brand team reviewed all existing quantitative data in order to establish some hypotheses about options for achieving future growth.

An important starting point was provided by a frequency of purchase analysis from a Usage and Attitude Study conducted at the end of 1977 (Table 9.1). Three-quarters of Flake buyers could be regarded as heavy purchasers, as they bought at least once a fortnight. These were the people we knew most about, the women who really loved the product and its advertising.

| | Percentage of | |
	Buyers	Volume
2/3 times a week	22	53
Once a week	34	33
Once a fortnight	20	10
Once a month	13	3
Every 2/3 months	6	0.5
Less often	5	0.5

Table 9.1
Frequency of purchase
(base: 470 Flake buyers)

103

But what about the other 24 per cent of our buyers, those who bought the product only occasionally — would there be an opportunity there to raise the 4 per cent of purchases they accounted for?

As well as looking at current buyers of Flake in this research study, we also interviewed non- and lapsed users of the brand to find out why they were not buying.

The reasons non-users gave for not buying broadly fell into two categories:

Too messy/crumbly	32 per cent
Dislike chocolate	18 per cent

These two reasons for non-purchase were also part of the motivation for purchase by our heavy and medium users. We concluded that it would be undesirable to change the actual product to satisfy this small group of consumers because we would risk losing our committed buyers.

We then examined reasons why the lapsed user had stopped buying the brand. This showed:

Too messy/crumbly	37 per cent
Prefer other bars	23 per cent

The reasons for preferring other bars were:

Better for sharing	99 per cent
More filling	30 per cent
Less messy	34 per cent

Flake is clearly not a brand for sharing — it is an individual self-indulgent treat. We concluded that it would be highly unlikely that we could turn these consumers back into Flake buyers.

Advertising strategy

We decided that the best way of arresting Flake's decline and increasing sales volume would be to persuade our light users to buy the brand more frequently.

Clearly they did not share the non-users' aversion to the product's primary characteristics, otherwise they would not have been purchasing the brand at all! The question thus became: how could we develop advertising that would convince this group to purchase in greater volume, without undermining the brand's current appeal?

Analysis of the TGI showed that the light user group was currently composed of 43 per cent men and 57 per cent women, with more than half falling into the 15—34 age group and a further 34 per cent in the 35—54 age bracket. The target audience was thus defined for us as potentially all adults with no particular age or sex bias. This represented an important departure as until now the advertising had been aimed essentially at women, with no conscious endeavour to attract men to the brand.

It was questioned whether our current advertising style was suitable for the task we had set ourselves of increasing purchase amongst these light users. Eventually it was decided that an alternative advertising campaign should be developed to achieve these difficult objectives.

Given that one of Flake's main strengths was its unique texture, it was decided that the competitive positioning should remain the same, that is:

'The milk chocolate bar with the unique texture.'

It was from this product-based positioning that an alternative creative strategy evolved.

From existing qualitative research we knew that the unique crumbly texture of Flake meant that the consumers developed their own 'ritual' for eating Flake in order to enjoy all the delicious crumbs of chocolate. We also knew that for some people, particularly light users, this crumbliness was seen as a negative; although they enjoyed the product they found the mess off-putting, and therefore they did not eat the brand as often as they might otherwise have done.

We decided that to motivate light users we had to acknowledge the crumbliness by tackling the 'messiness' problem head on, and turning the negative side of it into a positive. We thus arrived at a consumer proposition of:

'Every little piece of Flake is sheer enjoyment, so take care not to miss a morsel.'

Our new advertising objectives were defined as:

■ to dramatize single-mindedly the unique pleasure of eating the brand

■ to position Flake clearly as a brand enjoyed by a wide range of people.

We had now written an alternative strategy for Flake, one which significantly expanded the potential target audience. It introduced a proposition that continued to extol the virtues of the product's unique texture, but now also provided a stronger rationale for the potential negative.

Advertising development

Rarely can an advertising execution have flowed so smoothly from the strategy. The proposition 'every little piece of Flake is sheer enjoyment' and the idea of having to develop an art of eating the product were merged into a series of cameos. They showed a cross-section of people, as opposed to the archetypal Flake girl, capturing the last crumbs from a bar of Flake by various means – tipping back a chair, using a paper plate as a safety net and sucking up the last crumbs through a straw. The finished film 'Secretary' was researched amongst consumers using qualitative techniques. It performed very well amongst heavy, medium, light and lapsed users of Flake.

SECRETARY

Eating a Cadbury's Flake is no ordinary experience....

....in fact, there's an art to getting the most out of it....

....so the art is to capture every single crumb.

Yes, every bit of Flake is worth every bit of trouble it takes to eat it.

Alternative strategy: Secretary

Campaign

It was obvious that the decision about whether to replace a campaign which had run successfully for twenty years with one which had yet to prove itself was not going to be an easy one to make. A full research programme was needed in order to monitor the test for at least eighteen months to check that we had met all the objectives set for the test − that is, increased volume and higher frequency of purchase amongst light users, without alienating current heavy users.

It was decided to test the new strategy in approximately 25 per cent of the country, and to monitor results against the rest of the country.

London and the South were excluded, since a media test had been conducted in these areas during 1978, and the back data were therefore not comparable.

Lancashire and Yorkshire were eventually chosen, mainly because they provided an area which could be separately monitored in terms of ex-factory and depot sales. The control area was all other areas except London and the South.

The new film 'Secretary' was used in Lancashire and Yorkshire, and went on-air for the first time on 6 November 1978, while the current mainstream film 'Schooner' ran in the control areas. It was not felt that the particular mainstream film used should affect the test results, since in essence the Flake films were seen as one campaign, all featuring a girl, outside, alone, eating Flake with the familiar Flake theme tune.

Flake had a history of consistent television support, and it was decided to pursue a policy of equal impacts on all areas. Although this would cause difficulties in terms of television buying, since it would mean problems when area deals were being arranged, it was felt that this policy was imperative in order to ensure that unbalanced TVR levels did not affect the test.

Evaluation

As has already been emphasized, it was very much felt that the results of this test would determine the future strategy and executional style for the brand. Since everyone concerned was aware that we were testing a new strategy and execution which could well mean, if successful, that the history of twenty years advertising would be totally changed, it was agreed that the research used to track the test should be as comprehensive as possible, and that no final decision would be taken until sufficient data had been gathered to prove *conclusively* that the new strategy and execution would meet all the objectives set for the test − increased volume and higher frequency of usage amongst light users, without alienating current heavy users.

The research methods used to assess the performance of the test were comprehensive. Four different techniques were used.

AMTES (Area Marketing Test Evaluation System)

Format: A computer based system which is designed specifically to assess area tests. The system is capable of taking into account differences between areas in pricing, levels of TVRs, distribution and competitive activity. It predicts sales in the test area versus control, and this prediction can then be compared with the actual sales shift achieved.

Period: Data input from January/February 1976 to March/April 1980 (modelling period January 1976 − October 1978).

Objective: To measure the additional sales, if any, directly attributable to the copy change.

PPI (Personal Purchase Index)

Format: Diary panel of 10,000 individuals.

Period: September 1978 − February 1980 and 26 weeks ending February 1979 *v* 26 weeks ending February 1980.

Objectives: (a) to observe penetration levels and repeat purchase rates in the two areas (test and control). (b) To explore any change in demographics during the last period.

Tracking study

Format: 100 confectionery eaters interviewed every week.

Period: October 1977 onwards.

Objectives: To provide a continuous monitor of brand awareness, advertising awareness, campaign recall and brand image.

Surveys by Communication Research Ltd

Format: An *ad hoc* pre and post study amongst eaters of chocolate.

Period: Pre: week commencing 30 October 1978; Post: week commencing 21 April 1980.

Objective: To check recall and communication of the two campaigns amongst heavy and light users of Flake.

Results

The results of all four methods described above were positive. The highlights follow.

AMTES

Based on the eighteen months test data available to date — that is, since 'Secretary' had been on-air in Lancashire and Yorkshire — the best estimate of the effect of this area test on unit sales was an increase of 16 per cent on what would have been expected if the test had not taken place. The probability that the test had produced an increase in sales was greater than 99.9 per cent. There was a nineteen in twenty chance that the true effect of the test was delivering between +11 per cent and +20 per cent increase in sales.

PPI

A higher cumulative penetration was achieved in the test area. This meant that more buyers had been attracted to the brand:

Test area	26.4 per cent
Control area	21.6 per cent

In the test area buying was more frequent (Table 9.2). Also, males had been attracted to the brand in the test area, whilst the profile in the control area was unchanged (Table 9.3). Males were now accounting for 39 per cent of Flake's volume in the test area.

	Test 26 weeks ending:		Control 26 weeks ending:	
	Feb 79 (per cent)	Feb 80 (per cent)	Feb 79 (per cent)	Feb 80 (per cent)
Bought once	63	59	67	64
Bought twice	17	21	17	14
Bought once a fortnight or more often	3	5	1	1

Table 9.2
Frequencies of purchase

	Test 26 weeks ending:		Control 26 weeks ending:	
	Feb 79 (per cent)	Feb 80 (per cent)	Feb 79 (per cent)	Feb 80 (per cent)
Male	26	39	34	34
Female	74	61	66	66

Table 9.3
Sales breakdown by sex

Tracking study

Spontaneous awareness of Flake is at a similar level in both areas at about 25 per cent. Though claimed advertising recall is generally declining over time, this is mainly attributed to reduced advertising spend in both areas over recent years.

Total proven recall (that is, correctly recalling the execution among those who claimed to recall advertising for Flake) was much higher in the test area than in the control: test area 90 per cent, control area 75 per cent.

The only major difference in image between test and control was on the dimension 'would appeal more to women than men', where the control area response was much higher than in the test area.

Eaters of Flake in both areas equally regarded it as a treat and fun to eat.

We conclude from this that, in the crucial area of image, we had not shifted Flake's traditional image built up over twenty years. We were aware, of course, that it would probably take a long time to see any major shifts in image.

Ad hoc surveys

These were used to complement the tracking study and, unlike that study, provided measures at just two points at a time. However, special questions were added for this research only.

The increase in advertising awareness in the test area is shown in Table 9.4. Very high recall of 'Secretary' was found in the test area compared with levels achieved for the mainstream executions. 'Schooner' was on-air prior to 'Secretary', and 'Poppies' preceded 'Schooner'(Table 9.5).

The communication of 'Secretary' centred round the art of eating Flake in a positive way. Even light users did not feel that the film harmfully emphasized the messy aspects of eating the bar.

<table>
<tr><td></td><td>Pre
(per cent)</td><td>Post
(per cent)</td></tr>
<tr><td>Test areas</td><td>33</td><td>46</td></tr>
<tr><td>Control</td><td>34</td><td>36</td></tr>
</table>

Table 9.4 Advertising awareness

<table>
<tr><td></td><td>Pre
(per cent)</td><td>Post
(per cent)</td></tr>
<tr><td>Secretary</td><td>–</td><td>74</td></tr>
<tr><td>Schooner</td><td>21</td><td>2</td></tr>
<tr><td>Poppies</td><td>44</td><td>11</td></tr>
</table>

Table 9.5 Recall

Extension of test

Given this performance a cautious decision was taken to extend the test into London while continuing to monitor the performance of the new copy in Lancashire and Yorkshire, the original test market. In this case prudence proved to be the right course.

With the same research methods used to assess performance, similar findings were initially produced. AMTES, for example, concluded that a 23 per cent rise in London sales was attributable to the copy change. Panel data suggested that these gains had been caused by improvements in penetration among younger, lighter buyers who had now become a significant part of the Flake profile.

However, the same data now suggested a loss of 25–44 year old female repeat buyers, who were either dropping out of the brand entirely or else reducing the average weight of purchase. Examination of the original Lancashire and Yorkshire test market revealed the same trend, but in a more advanced stage. This loss of the 25–44 year old heavier buyers was only evident in the test areas, with this group remaining unaffected in the rest of the country.

Conclusions

■ One major conclusion from this test is the considerable gain that a copy change, and a copy change alone, can make in a brand's sales.

■ It is also evident that a copy change on a brand as well established as Flake can have considerable effect on the buyer profile, particularly in this case on the one demographic group of 25–44 year old women, the backbone of Flake and of the confectionery market as a whole. Alienation of this group is not something which can be taken lightly, even in the face of the significant sales increases and the recruitment of younger, lighter buyers. Previous experience with other brands had demonstrated that the younger light buyers can be fickle in their habits, either reverting back to old favourites or experimenting with the latest new brand on the market. Clearly a brand based increasingly on this franchise would be much less stable than one which drew its purchasers from the core of the market, the regular heavy user.

■ Changes to major elements of the marketing mix of a large brand should be monitored carefully over time to ensure that apparent opportunities, and even gains, really do augur well for the long-term future. Those charged with the stewardship of such major brands can, if they wish, produce substantial sales or profit effects through short-term changes. In this case it was through advertising copy. Advertising spend cuts and price increases can bring similar short-term benefits to profit. It is sustaining a long-term brand franchise that matters.

■ The final decision was to use the alternative film in a tactical manner only, extending its use into other areas in order to increase sampling among the light users. In the early test areas of Lancashire, Yorkshire and London the decision was to revert to the original campaign in order to retain the product's long-term appeal to the traditional target. After a limited period of use in the remaining areas, the alternative campaign will be once again replaced by the mainstream campaign, with research being used to monitor any signs of erosion of the long-term franchise in order to aid the decision on timings.

10
Kellogg's Super Noodles: Advertising's contribution to sales

Marketplace

We examine here the launch of Super Noodles, a completely new product from Kellogg. It shows how advertising has been a major component in the success of Super Noodles, both in the initial launch phase and also, with developments, through the important second year in the market, taking the brand to a value of over £5 million.

Early in 1978, Kelloggs had available a quick-cooking Japanese noodle product. There were many ways such a product could be packaged and positioned. Some manufacturers chose snacks as the opportunity, some the main meal. The noodles could be in a pot or a sachet. They could be an alternative to familiar foods or an exotic, foreign experience. They might be a children's food or suitable for all the family.

Research used group discussions and taste tests to explore various combinations of product form, packaging alternatives, names and concepts. The final recommendation was that the noodles should be a flavoured main meal accompaniment. Consumers found the product too bland to be consumed on its own as a snack, yet saw it as an acceptable part of a main meal, used, for example, as an alternative to potatoes.

				1977 £m RSP
Fresh potatoes				475
Instant potatoes				19
Packet pasta				13
Canned pasta				33
Packet rice				25
Savoury rice				5
Total				570

Sources: National food survey/Mintel

	1973	1974	1975	1976	1977
Smash	561	621	690	898	901

Source: MEAL

Table 10.1
Market size — Starch bulk meal components

Table 10.2
Smash adspend (£000)

From data like those in Table 10.1 we concluded that, if we could successfully position the product as a contender in this category, there was a large market opportunity.

The bulk of the market, fresh potatoes, was largely un-branded, yet successful entrants into the category — for example, Smash — had achieved success despite relatively high price, through consistent and heavyweight consumer advertising (Table 10.2)

For Super Noodles to succeed, the brand had to be clearly positioned with a competitive benefit against an established market category and consistently supported with heavy and strongly branded advertising communicating the desired positioning.

Additionally, the emergence in the test market of instant pot noodle products, marketed as snacks, meant that Super Noodles needed to be clearly differentiated from these products — as a main meal accompaniment. In fact, the competitive threat posed by the pot noodle products led to a decision to launch the Kelloggs brand nationally to pre-empt the pot products roll-out.

The marketing objectives of Super Noodles were:

■ to launch a major new non-cereal Kellogg brand in the UK worth £5 million at RSP within three years

■ to achieve volume sales in the first full year of launch of over nine million packs.

Advertising strategy

The overall advertising objective was to build awareness and trial for the brand, achieving 45 per cent awareness and 9 per cent trial by the end of the first full year of launch in order to generate the sales targets set.

It was clear from our initial product concept work that we needed to establish Super Noodles as a highly acceptable alternative to potatoes, in the context of a main meal eating occasion. Our targets were housewives who were receptive to convenience foods, particularly in terms of potato substitutes. Thus the full creative strategy was put together as follows.

Target audience. Housewives with children B, C1, C2 — particularly instant mashed potato users, who were attitudinally experimental.

Consumer proposition. New Kellogg Super Noodles are an exciting, easy to prepare alternative to potatoes.

Support. Noodles with special sachet of seasoning in a range of tasty flavours that cook in just four minutes.

Tone. Introductory, appetizing, modern, fun.

Advertising development

In order to set Super Noodles up as a delicious alternative to potatoes, we developed the idea of using an animated potato as a spokesperson, to extol the virtues of the new product. We pre-tested an animatic film, using individual interviews. We found we had a potentially impactful and credible creative vehicle allowing us to make claims for the product without in any way devaluing potatoes, which would have been incredible to consumers.

Small changes were made in the finished, animated film as a result of creative development research. The results showed we achieved clear communication of the positioning, with good branding.

Campaign

Budget

In order to help set a budget for the launch, we used the Leo Burnett Chicago new-product model. Based on considerable back data from new-product launches, this provides forecasts of likely awareness and trial achievements for given levels of television ratings. Given Super Noodles' awareness and trial objectives, a necessary strike rate could be determined from the model.

With the expected cost of this amount of air-time as a start point, and taking account of the three-year profit target, the budget was set at £1 million for the first year of national launch.

Media strategy

To make the launch highly visible and to maintain awareness of the product across the first full year of sale, a mixed media schedule was recommended, targeted at housewives with children. Television was recommended as the primary medium to provide rapid build-up of coverage, whilst women's magazines were used at launch to provide additional support, giving the opportunity for couponing and serving suggestions.

The television budget was estimated to deliver 1300 TVRs (thirty seconds) during the launch year. Given our desire to build rapid awareness, we aimed to use an opening television burst of six weeks (of 570 TVRs), in the autumn of 1979, supported by women's and general interest colour magazines. This was to be followed by four bursts of television activity during 1980.

In fact, the brand was launched coincidentally with the start of the ITV strike. Our launch media plans had to be substantially modified over the first three months, with money diverted into black and white press and posters, and only 190 TVRs achieved on television.

During 1980, however, the four television bursts were implemented as planned.

Evaluation

Super Noodles' in-market performance was closely evaluated during the first year of launch, using both *consumer studies* and *retail audit data* designed to provide a fast and accurate measure of the brand's standing. On the consumer side, *ad hoc* dip-stick tracking studies which could be reported quickly were fielded at strategic intervals to monitor awareness, trial and usage. On the retail side, Mars Group Services' continuous grocery audit was chosen to monitor sales and distribution, with data collected on a four-weekly basis and available within a week of measurement. These sales data provided the input for a statistical analysis to determine specifically the effect of advertising on the brand's performance.

The research showed that, after a disappointing start, with the advent of sustained television advertising Super Noodles performed extremely well, achieving preset sales and consumer targets. The analysis provided the evidence that advertising was indeed the main reason for the sales gains, and highlighted the fact that the brand was very advertising responsive, albeit in the short term.

The *ad hoc* **dip-stick tracking studies** were conducted by Public Attitude Surveys Ltd, amongst nationally representative samples of housewives in November 1979, and February, May and October 1980. They were timed to follow successive bursts of advertising.

The results showed that Super Noodles was very slow to respond over the period of initial press and poster advertising in the last quarter of 1979, but that with the start of television advertising in 1980 awareness and trial started to come through, and year-end targets were achieved (Table 10.3).

	Nov 79	Feb 80	May 80	Oct 80	Year 1 Target
Base: all housewives	1872 (per cent)	1292 (per cent)	1014 (per cent)	1063 (per cent)	(per cent)
Prompted brand awareness	22	36	45	42	45
Ever bought	5	9	8	10	9

	Nov 79	Feb 80	May 80	Oct 80
Base: Super Noodles ever bought	98 (per cent)	115 (per cent)	82 (per cent)	111 (per cent)
Bought once only	58	33	38	32
Bought more than once	42	67	62	68

Furthermore, amongst Super Noodle trialists, an encouraging level of repeat buying was reached during 1980 (Table 10.4).

Whilst at this stage the effect of advertising *per se* cannot be isolated, the consumer research did provide some clues as to how it might be working, with sustained television advertising clearly needing to communicate the desired meal accompaniment positioning. By the end of the first year of launch, trialists had understood how the product should be served, as can be seen from their claimed eating habits; but the direct impact of the advertising did appear to be weakening somewhat (Tables 10.5 and 10.6)

Base: Super Noodles ever bought	Nov 79 98 (per cent)	Feb 80 115 (per cent)	Oct 80 111 (per cent)
Claimed advertising awareness	45	58	48
Of which recall: 'Give potatoes a rest/ use instead of potatoes'	39	66	61

Table 10.5
Super Noodles advertising awareness and recall

Base: Super Noodles ever bought	Oct 80 111 (per cent)
How Super Noodles served:	
Meal accompaniment	**82**
Sausages	25
Chops/steak/mixed grill	17
Chicken	11
Beefburgers	8
Other meat	10
On their own	**18**

Table 10.6
Super Noodles serving patterns

Meanwhile, continuous retail audit data were providing further evidence as to Super Noodles' performance. Four-weekly sales off-take figures had been showing a poor performance against target in the last quarter of 1979, but the situation improved considerably with the advent of television support in the new year (Figure 10.1). By inspection, two key

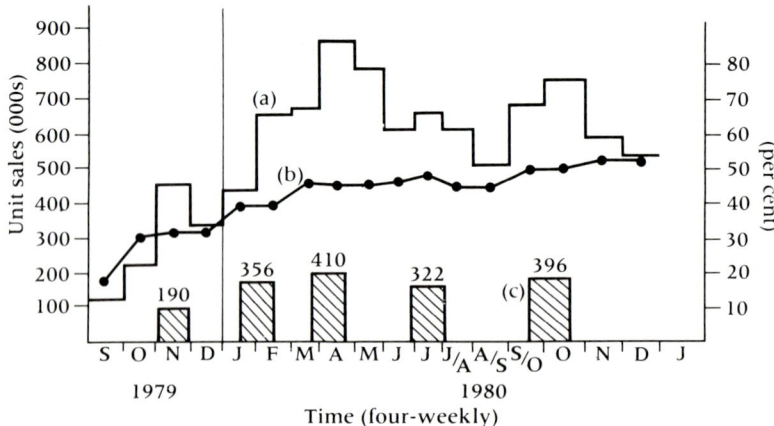

Figure 10.1   Super Noodles unit sales in the context of advertising and distribution, for 1979/80
(a) unit sales
(b) £ distribution
(c) TVRs

factors needed to be taken into account in evaluating Super Noodles' sales — *distribution*, where poor levels would certainly seem to have been hampering initial off-take, and *advertising support*, with each burst associated with an immediate and marked sales gain, which then fell away.

At this stage, with the data certainly suggesting a link between advertising and sales, a comprehensive statistical analysis was undertaken to provide evidence as to an advertising effect.

Statistical analysis

In order to provide a more definitive assessment of the effect of advertising on Super Noodles' sales, an econometric analysis of the data was undertaken. This involves developing a model of the market which sets out to establish the numerical relationship between the brand's sales and a number of variables which could have an effect on those sales, that is, short-term sales movements are 'explained' as a function of changes in outside factors, in the form of a simple algebraic equation

Brand sales = A × Advertising + B × Distribution + C × Price + D

The procedure involves computer analysis to find the values of the constants in the equation, to provide the best explanation or fit to actual historical sales data. Judgement and commonsense play a large part in deciding what factors might have an effect on sales, and hence what data to input. The computer analysis then determines whether the factors (singly or in combination) do have an effect, and of what magnitude, with the success of the operation being judged by how good a match the final model equation provides to sales data. In this way the effect of advertising can be isolated from the effect of other factors, and quantified.

The advertising effect itself can be described in terms of four key measures, which together provide an explanation of how advertising is working for the brand in question:

■ the proportion of sales movements 'explained' by advertising, and thus its importance in the marketing mix

■ the 'base' or residual level of sales estimated to exist when advertising support reduces to zero. This tells us about the extent of the longer-term or permanent effects of advertising and other factors

■ the advertising elasticity or short-term responsiveness of the brand, expressed as the increase in sales generated by a given increase in advertising level

■ the decay rate of the advertising, or how quickly the effect fades away. This is expressed as a 'half-life', or the time taken to reach half the total effect of the advertising.

The econometric analysis provides data on each of these measures, starting with the decay rate. The decay rate is used to spread the advertising notionally over time, to take account of the fact that it has both an immediate effect and a delayed effect in later time periods. This process of apportionment produces a measure of the effective amount of advertising in any given period (termed 'adstock'), and it is this which has to be used in deducing a direct relationship with sales in the full analysis.

For Super Noodles, the model was constructed using four-weekly Mars Audit Data on volume sales with an 'explanation' explored on the basis of three variables:

■ advertising (weekly thirty-second h/w TVRs converted to four-weekly adstock using an appropriate decay rate)

■ distribution (total effective £ weighted)

■ price (sales value divided by sales volume for price per unit, deflated by the RPI to March 1980 pence).

The time period chosen was one full year from the start of the television advertising with the launch 'Potato' execution (periods 1–13 in an analysis spanning February 1980 – January 1981).

The implications of this analysis in terms of Super Noodles' advertising effectiveness, deduced from the key values identified in the calculations, were as follows:

■ Super Noodles is a very advertising responsive brand:
(a)   advertising weight alone explained over 70 per cent of the variation in sales
(b)   in any given period, the degree of sales response achieved for increases in advertising was encouragingly high

(advertising elasticity = 0.31 compared with a norm of 0.2).

- The advertising effect has so far appeared to be short-term:
(a) there was a relatively fast rate of decay of sales response, such that the effect was half over in five weeks
(b) the base or residual level of sales was not showing signs of increasing over time, which would indicate a long-term, more permanent effect.

These findings were validated in the very good fit the model equation achieved in predicting actual sales (Figure 10.2).

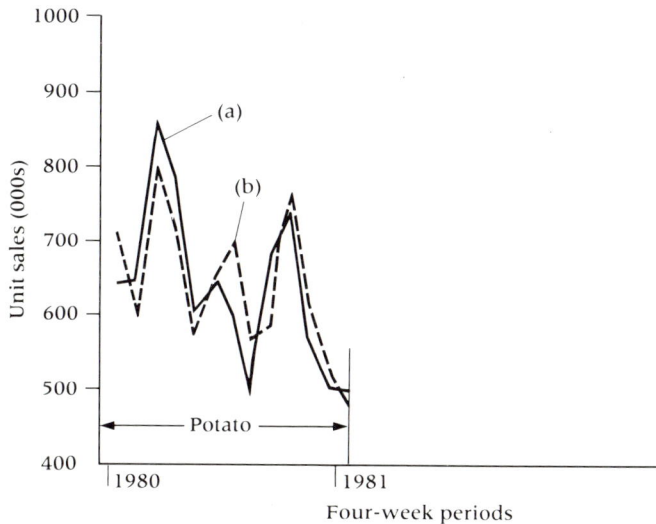

Figure 10.2 Model predictions versus actual sales (Potato) (a) actual (b) predicted from adstock alone

At this stage, therefore, analysis showed that advertising had a key role to play in the launch of Super Noodles, being a major contributor to sales during 1980. There was, however, evidence that it could be made to work even harder for the brand on a longer-term basis, if these sales gains were to be consolidated and built on in 1981 – a key requirement for continued success.

Development

Whilst the brand had made considerable progress by the end of 1980, it was clearly necessary to continue this momentum into 1981. The research and analysis already conducted to evaluate Super Noodles' performance served to provide guidance as to the brand's current position, and hence how best to exploit its potential further.

In order to build the brand, it was clearly necessary to increase penetration – but over and above that to develop a greater continuity of purchase. The first year's results suggested that Super Noodles was an advertising-led impulse buy. Therefore a key task for the second year would be to make the product part of an established repertoire of main meal accompaniments – a regular rather than intermittent purchase.

Overall, it was apparent that Super Noodles was still in the investment stage, and pressure (from distribution, advertising, point of sale efforts, etc.) must be kept up to develop its full potential for longer-term returns. All elements of the marketing mix were re-examined in the light of their contribution to building a sustained presence and interest in the brand, including the advertising.

With some evidence to suggest that the impact of launch advertising was diminishing, it was felt that new creative work was required. Further research was therefore conducted to explore the best way of developing the 'Give potatoes a day off' advertising route for the second year in the market. At this stage, however, it was found that a strategy setting Super Noodles up as an alternative to potatoes was no longer the best way to go. Whilst this was necessary at launch to position the product away from pot noodles, now the distinction was clearly drawn. Super Noodles needed to be established and built up *in its own right* as a different and delicious meal accompaniment, not just in the context of a (potentially infrequent) substitute for potatoes.

The consumer proposition was therefore changed to:

'Super Noodles are a different, delicious-tasting, convenient main meal accompaniment'

And a new execution dramatizing the product's appeal and versatility was developed with a broader based theme of:

'Add a new twist to mealtime'.

The experience of 1980 clearly indicated that television advertising had had a major impact on sales, but that further investment was required to maintain momentum and fully develop the brand's potential. Given Super Noodles' respon-

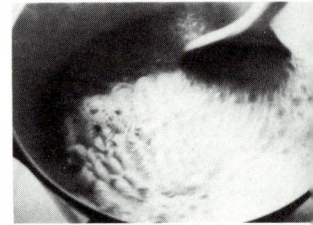

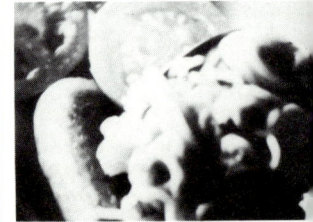

Twist those Super Noodles

122

siveness to spending on advertisements, with sales off-take increasing where the brand was stocked during a burst, it was felt that continued advertising support should lead to increased volume, provided that distribution improved and that the price to the consumer remained reasonable.

An increased media budget of £1.3 million was proposed for 1981, giving an estimated total TVR delivery of 1440 (thirty seconds). As regards laydown, the 1980 evaluation had shown a relatively fast decay rate for television advertising, which suggested that lengthy gaps between bursts should be minimized. In addition, the key objective of increasing the trial base necessitated a threshold strike rate across the country. The final plan provided for four bursts of 360 TVRs deployed throughout the year, with equal impacts across areas.

All the modifications to the marketing mix for Super Noodles, together with the proposed advertising and stocking support, were incorporated into a national plan. With all the evidence to date, it was strongly felt that the changes represented the best way forward for the brand, and that critical time would be lost if regional experimentation were undertaken. Overall, the total new 'package' was designed to generate a significant sales gain in 1981, and an ex-factory sales budget incorporating a 26 per cent increase over 1980 was laid down.

Given the ambitious growth strategy planned for the second year, it was important to continue monitoring the brand closely to evaluate performance in the light of various changes being made to the advertising. Similar methods of research and analysis were used. These showed a continuing successful performance for Super Noodles, with advertising again identified as a major contributor to sales gains. Furthermore, the new 'Twist' copy was shown to be working harder for the brand than the original 'Potato' execution in providing greater long-term benefits to Super Noodles.

On the launch budget index basis, it can be seen (Table 10.7) that ex-factory sales of Super Noodles in year two were significantly higher than those budgeted and achieved in year one. More importantly, shipments were ahead of target for 1981 despite an ambitious growth plan, providing considerable encouragement for the future.

	Budget 1980	Actual 1980	Budget 1981	Actual 1981
Ex-factory unit sales (indexed)	100	102	126	141

Table 10.7
Indexed ex-factory sales

Base: all housewives	Oct 80 1063 (per cent)	Mar 81 802 (per cent)	Sept 81 866 (per cent)	June 82 794 (per cent)
Prompted brand awareness	42	45	49	63
Ever bought	10	12	14	16

Table 10.8
Super Noodles awareness and

Base: Super Noodles ever bought	Oct 80 111 (per cent)	June 82 123 (per cent)
Bought once only	32	23
Bought more than once	68	77
Bought 2/3 times a month or more often	–	36

Table 10.9
Super Noodles repeat purchase

Tracking studies implemented at strategic post-advertising points over 1981/2 indicated that awareness and trial were growing steadily over this second year in the market (Table 10.8), with the repeat buying rate amongst trialists particularly encouraging (Table 10.9). All this was happening against a backdrop of the new 'Twist' advertising, and suggested that the brand was becoming a more established product in the housewife's buying repertoire.

The continuous four-weekly sales data showed clearly that Super Noodles' consumer off-take increased significantly in the second year of launch, with an overall year-on-year gain of 26 per cent over the period of the new television advertising.

As in 1980, a pattern of peaks and troughs can be seen which appeared to correspond to the presence or absence of advertising support (Figure 10.3). The relationship was now a little less clear by inspection alone, however, and the marked improvement in distribution levels (which finally achieved target) needed to be taken into account. Again, this formed the basis for a full statistical analysis to isolate the effect of advertising.

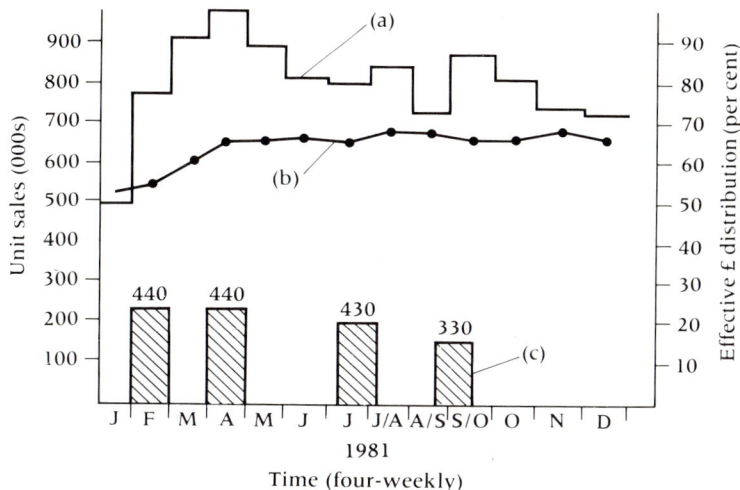

Figure 10.3 Super Noodles unit sales in the context of advertising and distribution, for 1981 (a) unit sales (b) £ distribution (c) TVRs

Statistical analysis

An econometric model applicable to 1980 data having been produced which provided a very good explanation of Super Noodles' sales, the first job was clearly to explore whether it was still relevant in explaining the sales gains achieved during 1981. Indeed, one of the ways of validating an econometric model is to examine its efficiency in predicting actual sales following the initial period of analysis.

From the model based on advertising alone, it can be seen that, in 1981, with new 'Twist' advertising, sales were significantly higher than would have been expected based on the performance of the original 'Potato' advertising alone – indicating that something was happening in the marketplace different from what had gone before, (Figure 10.4)

A new analysis was required which would explain what factors were affecting Super Noodles' sales in 1981; and to what extent, such that a comparison could be made with 1980. As before, the model was constructed using four-weekly Mars Audit Data on volume sales (actual sales shown above) – but this time two analyses were undertaken. One involved the time of the 'Twist' campaign alone, to check differences (periods 14–27 in the analysis, spanning February 1981 – February 1982), whilst the other used *all* the data available (periods 1–27), to provide a full and final explanation.

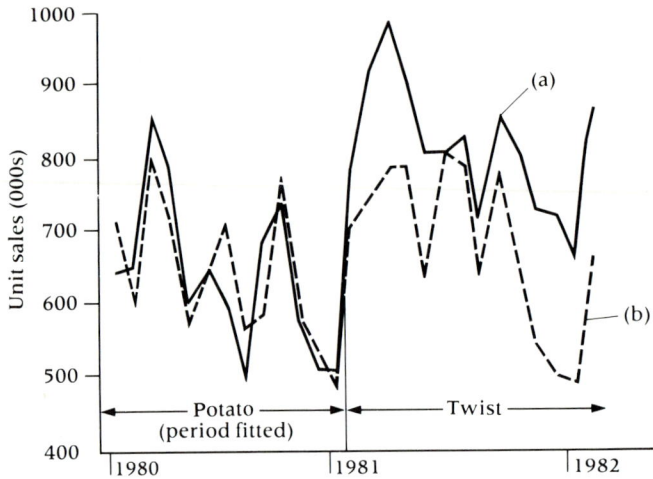

Figure 10.4 Model predictions (Potato) versus actual sales (Twist) (a) actual (b) predicted from adstock alone

The same three variables were used to try to explain sales, although new levels were operating in each case as indicated below:

■ advertising (new 'Twist' commercial and a higher TVR rate)

■ price (lower real prices)

■ distribution (raised to a higher level).

A full model was put together to cover the complete two-year period, with different advertising effects for each year as indicated above — but including constant factors for price and

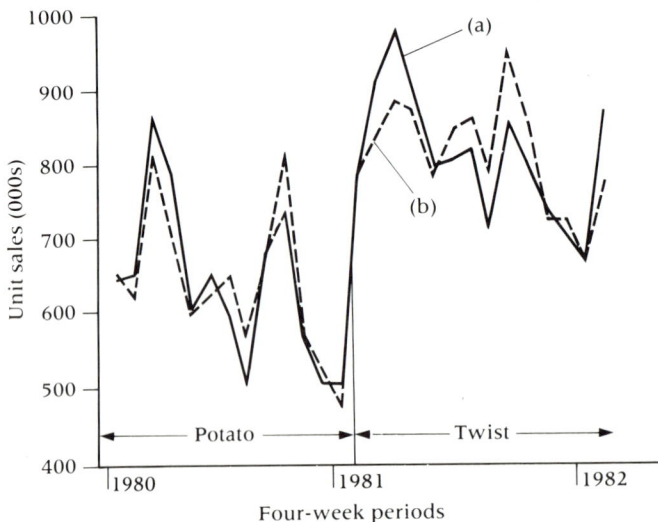

Figure 10.5 Model predictions versus actual sales (Potato and Twist) (a) actual (b) predicted from adstock, price and distribution

distribution elements. This combined model provided an excellent explanation of Super Noodles' sales, as shown by the fit of predicted to actual sales in Figure 10.5, and confirmed by the correlation of 0.84 with sales movements.

Overall, therefore, the analysis provided a very believable explanation of Super Noodles' sales over a period of growth and development, and was the means of isolating and quantifying the significant effect of advertising in the marketing mix.

Key findings

Super Noodles continues to be a very advertising responsive brand. Advertising was a major factor in the model, explaining over 60 per cent of the variation in sales. However, a fast decay rate was again evident, with a five-week half-life apparent for 1981, as well as for 1980.

Distribution and price were now needed as well to provide a good fit.

With the new 'Twist' commercial we made the advertising work harder for the brand than before. A higher base or residual level of sales was evident, indicating a longer-term or more permanent effect. At the same time, we were still obtaining a very satisfactory short-term response with an advertising elasticity of 0.2.

These findings suggest that Super Noodles was becoming more of an on-going regular purchase, rather than simply an advertising-led 'impulse' buy.

Conclusions

■ The launch of Super Noodles was a major success. Further, the brand has become an established going brand and the volume generated has been profitable.

■ We have shown the important role played by advertising in the first year of launch. Of perhaps even more interest, we have shown how modifications to the mix have resulted in an even greater success in the second year.

It is significant to note that, unlike many new-product launches, media investment was repaid by a worthwhile volume increase.

The brand achieved its three-year target of £5 million turnover by the end of the second year, and established for Kellogg a major introduction outside the cereal market.

■ A statistical model provided an excellent explanation of Super Noodles' sales, as shown by the fit of predicted to actual sales in Figure 10.5, and confirmed by the correlation of 0.84 with sales movements.

It was the means of isolating and quantifying the significant effect of advertising in the marketing mix.

11

The relaunch of Body Mist

Marketplace

Beecham Toiletries Group briefed us in September 1981 to review every aspect of Body Mist, their only deodorant brand and one which was showing significant share decline (Table 11.1).

Table 11.1
Body Mist: Percentage share (volume) of deodorants

1974	1975	1976	1977	1978	1979	1980
1.6	6.8	5.6	6.3	6.4	5.7	3.7

Source: Toiletries and Cosmetics Purchasing Index

Body Mist's history had been a very chequered one. Introduced by the Du Lundi Company in 1953 as a 'Perfume Substitute', it had been acquired six years later by the Beecham Group which, with the introduction of squeeze packs, had quickly made it brand leader. However, Body Mist did not respond so quickly to a product change in the 1960s, when it was a late entrant into the growing aerosol sector. Again, in the 1970s, when the anti-perspirant sector had been growing apace, Body Mist was late with an anti-perspirant formulation.

A major relaunch in 1977 successfully arrested the long-term share erosion, but further modifications in the brand's marketing mix, a change in fragrances in 1979, and revised, more feminine packaging in 1980, were unable to halt the brand's weakening market position. By 1981 Body Mist had been overtaken by Right Guard, Sure, Mum, Soft & Gentle, Arrid and Fresh 'n Dry.

This declining share was also to be viewed in the context of a market which, after huge growth in the 1960s and early 1970s, had become static. By the mid 1970s it was even showing slight decline. Penetration had now reached at least 80 per cent of women. Only seven out of ten men claimed to use a deodorant.

Only five out of ten could be described as regular users, but the opportunity of expanding this niche had been seized upon by brands from Beecham's competitors — 'Sure for Men' and the male-biased 'Right Guard' brand.

Consumers' perceptions of 'deodorants' had also greatly altered over this period of time. Previously considered to be a specialist, rather 'personal' product, the consumer had now become used to a wide range of available brands and was seeking to discriminate between them on a functional basis.

The Body Mist heritage ran contrary to this market trend. Based on qualitative research conducted in the late 1970s, Body Mist was found to be regarded as one of the original female deodorants, with a heavy perfume fragrance. Its image was feminine, old-fashioned, 'ethereal', passive and dainty, as it was attributed none of the effective properties of its rivals. Body Mist was being overlooked — it was no longer considered to be a candidate brand for many consumers' deodorant repertoires.

Body Mist had to be established anew as a candidate brand. Its penetration among our target audience had to be increased. Rejection had been perpetuated by the lack of new input to suggest change. Its ambivalent positioning, we felt, had been a major factor in its share loss. It had failed to fit neatly into any of the three sectors which had evolved in the deodorant/anti-perspirant market: *the unisex/family sector*, where a functional product was required; *the 'personal use' sector*, where effectiveness was key; and *the feminine/cosmetic sector*, which was now becoming largely the domain of the body sprays.

With the objective to regain brand leadership, two clear elements were outlined within the marketing strategy. The first was to *focus on the product's effectiveness to compensate for negative feminine characteristics*. The second was to *remedy the damage effected by the brand's disjointed marketing mix*.

Advertising strategy

Small-scale qualitative group research which we conducted in 1981 confirmed the findings of 1979 — that Body Mist lacked saliency and impact in today's deodorant market. We found that awareness of Body Mist advertising was extremely limited, and that Body Mist was thought to be a brand that *used* to be important but had become a brand with little real importance.

The key advertising task, therefore, was in creating awareness of Body Mist as a mainline deodorant with a real stature in the marketplace. We found that focusing on peripheral cosmetic benefits was rejected, and concluded that deodorant efficacy had to be the unequivocal basis of the Body Mist positioning.

Nonetheless, Body Mist's legacy as a feminine product was not ignored, and indeed could be harnessed as a positive element in repositioning the brand. Body Mist *was* firmly entrenched as a personal product for women — its name and heritage precluded it from adopting an asexual positioning. In fact, de-sexing Body Mist would not utilize its inherent strengths as a personal female product. Consequently, the recommended positioning was *the most effective deodorant for the personal use of women.*

To aid our decision on the key consumer benefit for the brand, fifteen advertising concepts, covering a wide range on a cosmetic-effective spectrum, were exposed to the consumer. These concepts covered both strategic and executional details and were designed to communicate a complete, and discreet, identity. Each of the concept boards carried a consumer benefit and support, an executional style and a rough packaging and graphic design to convey the intended mood of the various brand propositions.

It was found that the need to believe that a deodorant deals with sweat was overwhelmingly important. This was far more important than the precise nature of the benefit offered (for example, no smell, no wetness) or the rational explanations of the deodorant/anti-perspirant mechanism. Deodorants dealt with highly charged problems. These problems demanded powerful and potent solutions, and this had to be reflected in both the advertising benefit and the very tone of the message. For the potential purchaser of Body Mist, the brand had to present the most powerful solution against sweat.

A credible statement of change was essential to ensure impact and to convince consumers to reconsider the brand. The support for this new claim was provided by recent product reformulation carried out by Beecham — *Body Mist now contained less perfume to make more room for the ingredients that really fight sweat.*

Advertising development

Our concept research had also helped to identify the style of advertising which should be adopted. We wrote these as guidelines for the creatives.

The first of these guidelines dealt with the way to handle deodorant problems which are socially charged and potentially embarrassing. Humour, exaggeration or fantasy, it was felt could easily take the curse out of the situation and lend the benefit greater acceptability. In fact, we could be more convincing this way.

The second guideline dealt with the method by which to treat women in our advertising. Women 15—34 years old who are heavy purchasers of deodorants were our advertising target, and we had already come to the recognition that Body Mist's feminine imagery should be retained, albeit in a very different form. We believed that women would resist deodorants being treated as though they were cosmetic or perfume brands. Furthermore, women would recognize that the situations in which they sweated were active and vigorous and that deodorants should not be pampering and indulgent. Above all else, the deodorant must have the potency to deal with sweat. Femininity could be retained by simply featuring female users in the advertising and ensuring that the packaging and presentation of the brand clearly appealed to women.

Four advertising treatments on the new strategy were submitted to qualitative group discussions. These were presented to respondents as rough storyboards. They explored different areas for communicating the consumer benefit. 'Let the Men Perspire' showed a lady 'cool' among sweating men; 'Busy Day' which graphically described a girl's day speeding up; 'No Sweat' again featuring a girl, this time in sub-tropical conditions; and finally 'Don't Stand so Close' depicting, humorously, rejection and then acceptance by males.

Beecham then undertook exploratory qualitative research on two animatics. 'Don't Stand so Close' was found to communicate effects close to our strategic requirements; it was well-liked and found to be impactful by consumers. The contemporary beat of the 'Don't Stand so Close' music track by Police was very popular; while the vignettes that portrayed the before and after effects of using the brand seemed, as we had hoped, to turn potential embarrassment into enjoyment of the humorous style.

The centre section, featuring the pack, told the product story of 'less perfume ... more power' and communicated without being dissonant with the style of the advertising.

In summary, qualitative research showed that the animatic successfully communicated the power of Body Mist in providing social acceptability and attractiveness, with respondents appreciating the 'before and after' sequence.

Quantitative research by Millward Brown, undertaken for Beecham on the animatic in November 1981, endorsed these findings. It again confirmed the social acceptability story (16 per cent mentioning) and reassured us that the vital communication of product change was being conveyed credibly and strongly. Seventeen per cent of the respondents played back 'effective/efficient/works better' while 15 per cent played back the product change communication. Also, 74 per cent of respondents said they liked something about the 'Don't Stand' commercial, with music and humour the main elements of this approval. 'Don't Stand' also obtained a high level of endorsement for the statement 'I would like to see it again on TV at home' (49 per cent), and we were encouraged by the 39 per cent who said it was an interesting commercial.

In our music track, we had an execution that could be taken to radio. In the brash, modern style we had created, with the 'pre' and 'post' cameos of social rejection and then acceptance, we could also foresee further television executions. Moreover, the copy line, 'Don't stand so close', was already providing a strong theme idea for the packaging, promotion and merchandising departments. Importantly, the line 'Now you can stand closer...' successfully encapsulated both the deodorant efficiency message and also a statement of change. 'Don't stand so close', we were confident, was campaignable, and could provide us with both the immediate results we needed and the long-term change in brand imagery which we knew Body Mist required if it were to successfully regain and hold its lost share.

The shoot in early January 1982 was designed to provide us with a pool of thirty-second commercials, with possible twenty-second cutdowns for use later in the campaign. A total of seven 'vignettes' (gym, umbrella, archery, swimmers, thinker/statue, ballet, boxers) were shot in the studio and edited into two initial thirty-second commercials.

Final qualitative research (Research Business: March 1982) using an in-depth interview technique was then conducted among twenty-four respondents. This evaluated the reactions to the two finished commercials and the individual vignettes featured in each. Once again spontaneous positive reaction was very high. The beat of the music, in particular, helped enormously. The poetic licence in the style and presentation of the advertising was well accepted. Reactions to the individual vignettes varied considerably — some respondents thought they were totally unrealistic, dramatic and exaggerated; while some respondents voiced doubts whether this made them less believable or more effective in adding impact to the commercials. The agency felt strongly that the over-dramatization in the vignettes was vital in achieving the necessary impact.

During this period of advertising development, from October 1981 to March 1982, the second aspect of the marketing strategy — to form a cohesive marketing mix for Body Mist — was also being met.

A change in name had been decided. The brand would now be Body Mist 2, to convey to the consumer a real and meaningful change.

'Stand close...'

134

Stand close with Body Mist 2.

Packaging graphics had been radically altered to meet the new marketing positioning, that of 'the most effective deodorant for the personal use of women'. The design became simple, clean, losing any fussy femininity while still retaining a feminine appeal through the choice of soft green/red/blue tones to mark the individual variants.

'Lighter fragrance' had been introduced as an on-pack claim which provided a rationale for the product change. A performance-based claim of 'keeps you really dry' had also been introduced. The previous variant colours had been replaced with a plain white background to help communicate a fresh, clean image. Two final pieces of research satisfied both client and agency that the new packaging look would help to make the brand more relevant to a functional, efficacy-based market, while sacrificing nothing in on-shelf standout.

Packaging construction also aided this overall new look. Trimline aerosol cans were used with a cap embossed with the brand name. Pack copy was rewritten to echo the message of the advertising... 'Now you can stand closer with New Body Mist 2 ... Less perfume. More power'.

Campaign

The weight of advertising behind Body Mist 2 obviously had to convince both the trade and consumer that Beecham really had effected a radical change.

Market advertising spend had increased significantly over the previous four years with the introduction of body sprays and their advertising-led propositions. The 'established' deodorant market spend had moved from £2,992,000 in 1978 to £5,843,000 in 1981, a slight decline in real terms. Body Mist's spend had been considerable in 1978–80; but copy had shifted over the years and, indeed, all brand advertising funds had been withdrawn in 1981. Competition, meanwhile, had maintained a high level of investment (Table 11.2).

	1978 £000 (per cent)		1979 £000 (per cent)		1980 £000 (per cent)		1981 £000 (per cent)	
Body Mist	384	(13)	120	(6)	594	(13)	–	–
Right Guard	700	(23)	569	(28)	1040	(23)	694	(12)
Sure	320	(11)	330	(16)	410	(9)	1131	(19)
Mum	322	(11)	195	(10)	637	(14)	481	(8)
All brands	2992		2034		4555		5843	

Source: MEAL

Table 11.2
Adspends for leading brands

The agency had projected a likely 1981 spending on advertising of £5,300,000, given a similar market state to 1980 but assuming 15 per cent media inflation. In fact, it was £5,843,000 moving to £6,100,000 in 1982. Given this increase and a share of voice objective of 14 per cent for Body Mist – double its projected sales share – a media budget of £840,000 on *Meal* rates was agreed.

Television was an obvious candidate for media selection. It would quickly re-establish the brand to both the trade and consumer and ensure visibility as a deodorant advertiser.

Analysis had told us that the market had strong 'advertising' seasonality, despite the comparative flatness of sales across the year. Indeed, about 90 per cent of the spending on advertising was put against 37 per cent of the sales in 1980.

	J/F	M/A	M/J	J/A	S/O	N/D
Consumer sales (index)	75	84	101	119	110	113
Advertising spend (index)	–	7	190	354	46	4

Table 11.3
Deodorant category seasonality

We had to balance (a) the need for a noticeable relaunch burst, (b) the opportunity to advertise ahead of the pack and at a time of good value, and (c) our wish to cover as much of the year as possible, without diffusing the initial launch impact or neglecting the need to reassure the trade that we were supporting the traditional 'deodorant' season. The campaign, deployed over the period April to August, delivered 700 TVRs with an estimated cover of 87 per cent and frequency of eight opportunities to see.

Our second concern touched our requirement to reach the target audience of 16–34 year old women cost-effectively. Recognizing that this target was characterized by their light viewing habits, a special buying strategy, with a balance of programming between the mass coverage slots, such as 'Coronation Street', and the lower rating late-night midnight films, was adopted.

A wide range of below-the-line activity to stimulate trial of new Body Mist 2 was planned to coincide with the commencement of the campaign. An attractive laydown price was offered at launch, flash-marked packs were available during the first three-month period, an aggressive promotional programme of added-value packs was planned, and banded packs were offered to key selected outlets to generate repeat purchases.

The Beecham salesforce themselves were well equipped for the launch. Special pens, gift-sets and sweat shirts were dispensed, all carrying the simple 'Stand close ... with Body Mist 2' message. The trade had been advised of the launch well in advance and their advice carefully followed.

Evaluation

Relaunch business results were speedy.

Consider first ex-factory case sales. From an average monthly level of 500,000 cases, sales quickly rose to over 600,000 in March, then to a further 800,000 cases by June. By September an all-time high of over one million cases had been achieved. Thus deliveries of Body Mist had doubled.

Year-end figures (April 1982 – April 1983) showed a gratifying 47 per cent volume rise over the previous years. Trade reports were encouraging and repeat orders had been secured. There is no sign of a fall-off in the brand's rate of sale.

Consumer off-take matched these increases. In 1980 and 1981 the brand averaged 4 per cent share (TCPI). At the peak of the relaunch (July/August) this doubled to 8 per cent.

A Beecham continuous tracking study also showed the increases that the above-the-line investment had wrought on brand and advertising awareness. Brand awareness grew from 15 per cent in January to 25 per cent in July 1982; while advertising awareness increased from 5 per cent to 13 per cent over the same period. 'Used nowadays' also grew.

The way these measures moved period by period provides interesting confirmation of our adstock model. As usual, we took advertising awareness as the variable to fit in estimating the half-life of our advertising, since this is usually uncontaminated by other factors.

Figure 11.1 shows the way this measure moved. Our TVR laydown, week by week, is also shown. We decided on a five-week half-life and the adstock which was calculated is given in the figure.

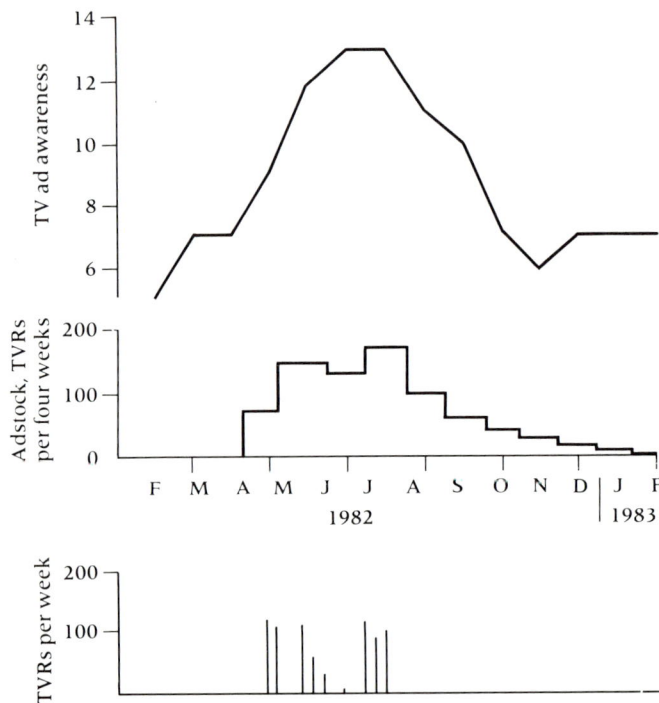

Figure 11.1   Body Mist

Fitting the observed data was clearly successful; our correlation coefficient was 0.9. Figure 11.2 gives the observations again, and the prediction using the equation:

predicted $= 7 + 3.3 \times$ adstock.

Thus we had a good estimate for the effectiveness of our advertising (in creating awareness) which we could use in predicting the results of further advertising.

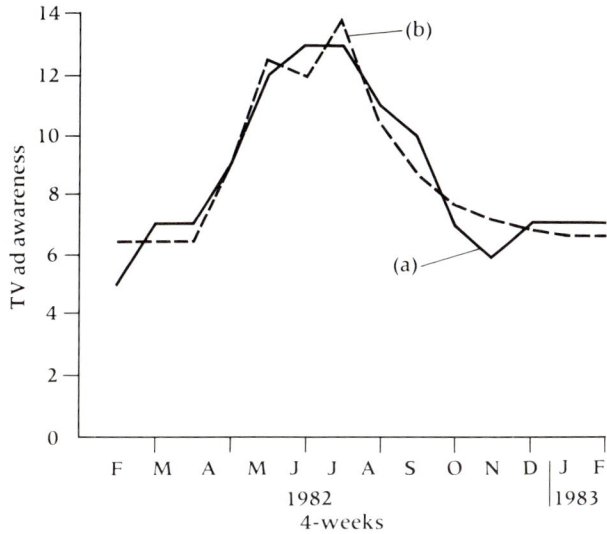

Figure 11.3 shows how the other two tracking study measures moved – again closely related to adstock. In fact they are well predicted by the following fits, with correlations of 0.75 and 0.69:

brand awareness = 18 + 3.0 × adstock
used nowadays = 15 + 2.0 × adstock.

At the peak, ten percentage points were added to brand awareness and six to claimed usage. Even when the immediate

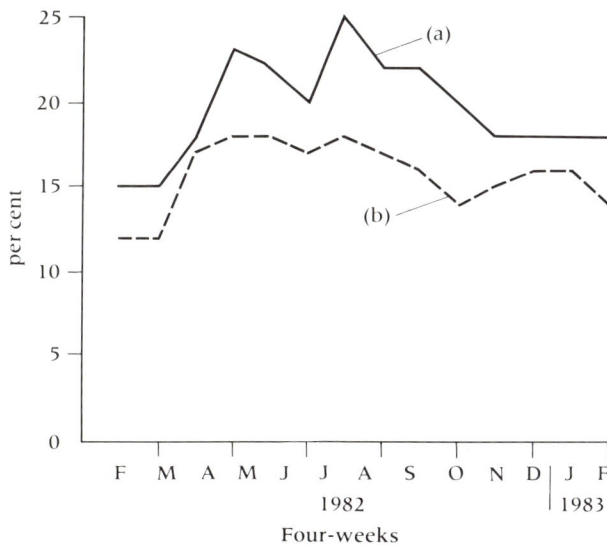

effects are over, brand awareness and usage are both three points above pre-campaign.

Conclusions

This was a successful relaunch. It impressed the retail trade and, closer to home, has confirmed that a declining brand *can* be turned about. It also proves four important points:

■ *A brand with a clear existing image can be successfully repositioned in a changing market.* An old brand can be successfully brought up to date without a complete emasculation of all the heritage and franchise that it had built up over the years. Negative aspects, such as that presented by Body Mist's fussy frilliness, could be made positive by careful strategic thought.

■ *A relaunch needs to be underpinned by a real product improvement,* capable of being appreciated by the consumer. Body Mist's increased efficacy was the cornerstone of the projects.

■ *A thorough and cohesive marketing mix is essential.* The benefits of the improved product and the more modern image it conferred was communicated clearly and single-mindedly through all aspects of the marketing — advertising, packaging (graphics, variants, descriptions and pack copy), consumer promotions and trade and salesforce communications.

■ *The effect of advertising on consumer perceptions was clear* in tracking study data and could be successfully modelled, helping future planning.

12

Lucozade: real brands don't die

Marketplace

The launching of new products may seem more glamorous and exciting, but the relaunching of old ones is very often more rewarding financially. It can also be a much tougher task. Ingrained consumer perceptions and attitudes about the brand must be shifted by advertising before progress can be made.

The life cycle theory of brands has some evidence to substantiate it: if you do not revitalize a brand it will die. If this had not happened to Lucozade, it would be dead and buried by now. Launched in 1927 by a chemist in Newcastle, it surely must have had its day. Yet the fact that Lucozade is still a vigorous and buoyant brand is proved by its major profit contribution to Beecham Foods. Housewives today buy Lucozade, not out of affection for an aged institution, but because it has a real and useful role that continues to grow.

A major reason for the brand's health today comes from a repositioning of Lucozade conducted in 1977/8. This chapter examines the thinking behind the repositioning and sets out its effects.

Viewed over the long term Lucozade sales had declined from an all-time high of 5 million dozen bottles a year in the mid-1950s to 3 million dozen in the mid-1970s. All the indications were that this decline would continue.

Lucozade as a product is a carbonated glucose drink. The glucose content is a highly concentrated source of food energy which is quickly and easily absorbed into the blood. It is particularly appropriate to take when one is ill since it is a ready source of nourishment that requires little digestion.

However, Lucozade's properties are not relevant only to convalescence. Its citric flavour and light carbonation make it a refreshing drink in its own right. A 20 ml glass of Lucozade provides sufficient food energy for a healthy person to run upstairs non-stop − if the notion took him − for thirteen minutes.

The problem was that these wider attributes were not being communicated to Lucozade's main purchasers, who were housewives.

Instead, a number of factors were conspiring to drive Lucozade's sales down. This sales decline had begun to accelerate; sales fell 12 per cent in 1976/7, so that the problem now required urgent action.

In considering this sales decline, the following seven major causes were identified.

Housewives' reasons for buying Lucozade

Advertising had consistently positioned Lucozade throughout the 1960s and 1970s as a brand for convalescence. This consistency of approach was rewarded by a shift in house-wives' attitudes to the brand (Table 12.1) To have achieved a figure of 84 per cent of all housewives buying Lucozade was, on the face of it, very satisfactory.

Lucozade aids recovery

Closer examination, however, revealed that most of these were very light purchasers indeed. In fact 46 per cent of housewives accounted for only 18 per cent of the volume.

	1968	1971	1974
Convalescence	48	59	61
Pregnancy	4	8	11
Refreshment	6	5	4
Other	4	6	2
Ever bought	62	78	84

Source: Beecham U & As

Declining sickness levels

A key reason for the marked infrequency of purchase was a decline in sickness levels over the 1970s.

The quantity of doctors' prescriptions and of sickness benefit claims over the last ten years were analysed. Two facts clearly emerged.

- The population was getting healthier – sickness levels were falling.

- Whilst 'flu epidemics still occurred, fewer people were suffering.

A combination of better diet and medical care was significantly reducing the occasions when people were convalescent. If use in convalescence was Lucozade's key reason for purchase, this was a problem.

Changing consumer attitudes

In fact, even if sickness levels had been stable, it was likely that Lucozade's use as an aid to recovery would have fallen.

Housewives' attitudes to paramedical, self-medication products were becoming a good deal more sceptical than in the immediate post-war years, and criticisms were to be heard increasingly that Lucozade was no more than a patent nostrum. Whilst this was not true, it nevertheless contributed to the sales decline.

Price

An altogether more important reason for the immediate sales

decline was price. After a period of relative price stability in the early 1970s, Lucozade became affected by the pressures of inflation. By 1976/7, its price, unfortunately, had begun to rise faster than the retail price index. (Table 12.2). Clearly, such price increases were not helping sales.

	RPI	Lucozade
72/3	+8	−2
73/4	+12	+8
74/5	+27	+20
75/6	+17	+16
76/7	+16	+26

Source: Monthly Digest, Beecham Foods

Table 12.2
Percentage price change versus previous year

Retail distribution

Twenty per cent of Lucozade volume is sold by chemists and 80 per cent through grocers. However, Lucozade's grocery trading profile was not following the same pattern as other major food and drink brands. One would normally hope to see at least 40 per cent of volume coming from the dynamic and rapidly growing multiple sector. In Lucozade's case this was only 20 per cent, with the remaining grocery volume coming from symbol groups and independents.

   Although clearly not the major cause for any volume decline, this was identified as a situation for concern.

Sales force

Sales force attention is traditionally concentrated on areas of high volume and excitement, and for the Beecham Foods sales force this was provided by an extensive range of canned and bottled soft drinks. Lucozade, on the other hand, although more profitable to the company than soft drinks, sold very much lower volumes.

Advertising

Finally, there was the question of advertising. The increased irrelevance of our strategy has already been described − that is, the advertising positioned Lucozade firmly as an aid to recovery from sickness, whilst sickness levels were falling.

   Just as important was the issue of advertising weight.

Lucozade's business has been built with the help of television. A succession of analyses exist which demonstrate television advertising's positive effect on sales.

Unfortunately, the price of television airtime began to rise rapidly at the time that Lucozade's volume sales started their more rapid decline. This coincided with a number of short-term company profit requirements which led to advertising expenditure declining. The conjunction of these factors had a marked effect on the television ratings that Lucozade could afford (Table 12.3).

	Housewife TVRs	Volume sales (1970 = 100)
73/4	3796	123
74/5	3554	121
75/6	2806	120*
76/7	2062	105

Table 12.3
Declining TV support

* Year with high sickness

Whilst 3796 thirty-second housewife ratings seems an unattainably high level by today's standards, this had definitely been associated with strong sales. Reduced advertising pressure went with lower sales.

Advertising strategy

Anyone faced with the problems on Lucozade that existed in 1977 could be forgiven for considering other careers. The brand was in decline. Its advertising was being cut. Its price was rising ahead of inflation. Fewer people were falling ill. Most purchasers were light users.

Yet all was not lost. Beecham had commissioned a Usage and Attitude Study that proved to be an especially rich source of information. The most revealing area concerned who bought, in what volumes and for what purposes.

The first surprise was that, whilst the majority of purchasers were buying for convalescent children, they did not account for the majority of the volume. In reality, adult women were the key consumers (Table 12.4).

Table 12.4
Drinker volume (per cent)

Adult female 16+	50
Adult male 16+	20
Children 0−15	30

The second surprise was the reason for 70 per cent of volume being bought for adults. Most were drinking the brand either as a refreshing drink or as a pick-me-up (Table 12.5).

Purchase frequency	Household (per cent)	Volume (per cent)	Purpose (per cent)
Heavy (at least once per week)	5	50	Refreshing drink, tonic
Medium (at least once a month, less than once a week)	9	32	Pick-me-up, minor sickness
Light (at least once a year, less than once a month)	46	18	Sickness, convalescence

Table 12.5
Proportion of consumption and purpose

These figures challenged long-cherished beliefs. The clear conclusion was that adults, women in particular, were the major users of the brand, and that convalescence was not its only use.

In consequence, even if the sales decline was partly due to the fall in sickness levels, there was still a very healthy part of the brand's volume which did not depend on illness. If only more healthy people would be persuaded to drink the brand, the sales decline could be halted.

Conversely, the worry was that any over-vigorous repositioning of the brand as a drink for healthy people could well lose the remainder of the important child convalescence usage. A more subtle approach was needed. We can summarize these conclusions as follows:

■ Same strategy, but improve execution: do not desert bedrock of brand.

■ Extension strategy with new intrusive execution: look for greater usage, and remember trial comes from sickness.

■ New strategy for in-health usage: research identifies need for housewife pick-me-up.

From this initial consideration, four positioning concepts were prepared. It was clear at this early stage that qualitative research was needed. The technique chosen was in-depth interviews, twenty-four respondents being selected who covered a spectrum of Lucozade usage.

The objective of the research was to establish if Lucozade could be repositioned to encourage consumption in both sickness and health. Briefly, the results were:

Concept	Response
'Helps a child get better'	No more than a reminder of how Lucozade was currently perceived.
'Golden sparkling reviver'	Appealed to light and lapsed users, but made heavy users think of sickness.
'Refreshment plus glucose energy'	Appealed strongly to heavy users as an excuse to continue using the product. Light and lapsed users were unclear what job the glucose was supposed to perform.
'Refreshing drink'	Not appealing since it made Lucozade seem like a fizzy drink.

What was clear was that either 'golden, sparkling reviver' or 'refreshment plus glucose energy' could generate more volume and that there was hope in this route. However, both had their shortcomings. What was needed was an expression which would reinforce heavy users in their consumption patterns whilst encouraging the more frequent light users to become heavy users.

The simplest way to do this would be to convince those who were already disposed to believe the product's usefulness outside the sickroom to use it more frequently. The target was therefore housewives who were heavy and medium users of Lucozade, and the initial proposition:

'Lucozade is a refreshing and everyday source of glucose energy.'

It now needed to be proved that an everyday usage for Lucozade could be communicated in a believable and motivating way. A further stage of research was needed for this, and it was decided that the best way of handling this was to run a series of group discussions which focused on twelve propositions. Once more, these propositions covered a spectrum of possible claims:

'Lucozade is liquid glucose that is more easily digested than food.'

'One glass of Lucozade has the energy equivalent of one large egg.'

'One glass of Lucozade can give you enough energy to climb stairs non-stop for thirteen minutes.'

'Lucozade energy is absorbed twice as fast as food energy.'

'Lucozade is glucose energy in the fastest form the body can take.'

'The first sip starts working before you finish the glass.'

'Lucozade is pure, natural body energy.'

'Lucozade restores energy faster than food.'

'Lucozade has the energy to keep your body going strong.'

'When you're hungry for energy...'

'Lucozade has the energy to put some sparkle back into your family.'

'Lucozade restores your energy rate.'

The last six of the concepts had accompanying body copy.

Some of the propositions may seem to have a tenuous link with reality, but this is how we discover the limits of consumer belief. The general conclusions of the groups were:

■ Everyday pick-me-ups do exist in a variety of forms, including tea, Mars Bars, Kit Kats and coffee. Lucozade could credibly fit this role.

■ Lucozade should not be associated with food energy, speed of action or improper diet.

■ The role of Lucozade is one of restoring to normality rather than giving extra energy.

■ The 'energy rate' concepts offered the best potential.

The 'energy rate' concept board was illustrated by a line from an oscilloscope. The body copy simply said: 'When your body gets tired, your energy rate drops. Lucozade works fast to restore the body's energy supply and get you going again.'

This particular concept struck a number of sensitive chords.

First, it sounded believable. Many of the women in the group commented that looking after a family and running a house involved hard physical work, and that they did need a pick-me-up from time to time when their energy flagged.

Second, it provided a reason for light consumers to drink the product more often. Third, it confirmed heavy users in their usage. And finally, it did not conflict with use in convalescence.

Now we knew that we could credibly and motivatingly communicate a wider usage for Lucozade. The job that advertising would have to do was all the more important since neither the product nor the packaging was to be changed. Further, the advertising had to widen usage of Lucozade without alienating its applications to sickness. Thus the proposition changed subtly:

'Lucozade helps the body regain its normal energy level...'

with the justification:

'...because its glucose energy is energy in the most natural form the body can use.'

Advertising development

It proved surprisingly easy to write advertising to the new strategy.

Four campaigns were prepared which ranged from a slice of life to a presenter, and from a documentary style to the use of the oscilloscope line from the 'energy rate' concept.

Lucozade: Ups and Downs

All four scripts were researched qualitatively and quantitatively. None of them failed in the primary task of communicating the replacement of lost energy. One of them, however, based on the 'energy rate' concept, performed particularly well.

By now it had been rewritten as a commercial focused specifically on recovery from feeling tired during the course of the day, and was entitled 'Ups and Downs'. It was this commercial that we eventually shot, and the reasons for this were as follows:

- The advertising had a strong idea in the form of an orange line depicting tiredness and activity.

- This orange line was well-integrated with the action.

- The story was convincing and well understood.

- The combination of animation and live action was visually intriguing.

The 'Ups and Downs' commercial was first aired in July 1978 after a year's intensive work.

Campaign

The media objectives were to create maximum awareness of the new Lucozade usage opportunities as quickly as possible, and to maintain these levels of awareness as long as possible.

Achievement of these objectives required a burst of television advertising at the start of the repositioning. The television weight dropped to under half the initial burst weight later on in the plan, but maintained advertising over as long a period as we could afford.

A women's press campaign began six months after the launch. This carried the traditional convalescence message to reinforce the roots of the brand, but in a media environment away from where we were concentrating the in-health advertising.

During the second half of the year posters were used to provide extra frequency of impact for the television in-health message.

As the trade viewpoint was identified as a problem, a sales force and retail trade package was put together to tie in with the new advertising:

On-pack promotion
Special 12-minute film for key account buyers
Special sales force material explaining the rationale for the change.

A new quarter-litre wide-mouth bottle of Lucozade was introduced to reinforce out-of-home consumption by healthy people. Later in 1982 a one-litre bottle was introduced alongside the traditional 25 oz bottle, to capitalize on volume opportunities at the top end of the multiple trade.

Evaluation

Although we changed nothing else deliberately, unquestionably factors other than advertising do affect the market. A problem is how to disentangle the influence of advertising from all other factors. In order to make this assessment, the decision was made to leave the old convalescence advertising in the Tyne Tees area and use Beecham's Area Marketing Test Evaluation System (AMTES) to gauge what success the new advertising produced over what may have happened in the marketplace.

The AMTES conclusion was that an 11 per cent volume sales increase was directly attributable to the change in advertising in the six months of the test. This should be compared with a volume sales increase of 21 per cent overall for the period. Clearly, nearly half of the sales increase observed was due to factors other than the change in advertising.

Following the repositioning advertising, a regular Usage and Attitude Study went into the field. While no dramatic results were expected at an early stage, a number of movements in a positive direction were recorded.

- a significant increase in claims to buy Lucozade 'nowadays'

- a significant increase in strong likelihood of 'ever buyers' to repurchase

- a significant increase in the recall of Lucozade television advertising

- most gratifyingly, a significant increase in claims to purchase Lucozade for 'refreshment' reasons among frequent purchasers.

The acid test of a change in strategy is its effect on national sales in the marketplace after the launch of the new advertising. In sharp contrast to the previous severe volume decline of the brand, volume sales increased by 13 per cent in the first year.

The chequered earlier history has been replaced by steady sales volume. At the same time, positioning has allowed price rises above inflation, with a healthy effect on profits (Table 12.6).

	Price deflated by RPI to 1978/9 prices/	Volume sales (1970 = 100)
1978/79	40.0	110
1979/80	42.0	106
1980/81	45.2	106
1981/82	46.0	109
1982/83	46.3	108

Table 12.6
Sales over time

Finally, our analysis has been able to uncover five major factors which are associated with Lucozade sales volume over this period. These are:

■ sickness levels (the trend, the seasonal peaks and the occasional 'flu epidemic all have effects)

■ real personal disposable income (when money is short, Lucozade sales suffer)

■ real price (for a similar reason)

■ advertising weight (the adstock model described above shows that recent advertising has an effect)

■ advertising content (the repositioning is left as the major reason why sales since 1978/9 have been steady, despite the adverse trends in other factors).

Development

Following this first evidence of success, further commercials using the 'orange line' idea were run. A tactical convalescence commercial, to be aired in the winter, was included in the pool. The campaign matured and maintained its effectiveness.

The campaign's major achievement was to shift people's attitudes and take Lucozade from exclusive use in sickness to use in health. Because this largely succeeded, more vigorous settings for the use of Lucozade could be envisioned. The thought evolved that Lucozade might benefit from being shown as being an especially refreshing and appropriate accompaniment to hard physical activity. This could be an effective way of further widening the brand's appeal, and could be done in an especially effective and arresting fashion.

The decision was therefore taken to move the campaign forward by using a sports personality in conjunction with Lucozade. The man chosen was Daley Thompson who, at the time, was the Decathlon world record holder. He won the Gold Medals at the 1980 Moscow Olympics and the 1982 Commonwealth Games. Voted BBC Sports Personality of the Year, he was to be a powerful ally for the brand.

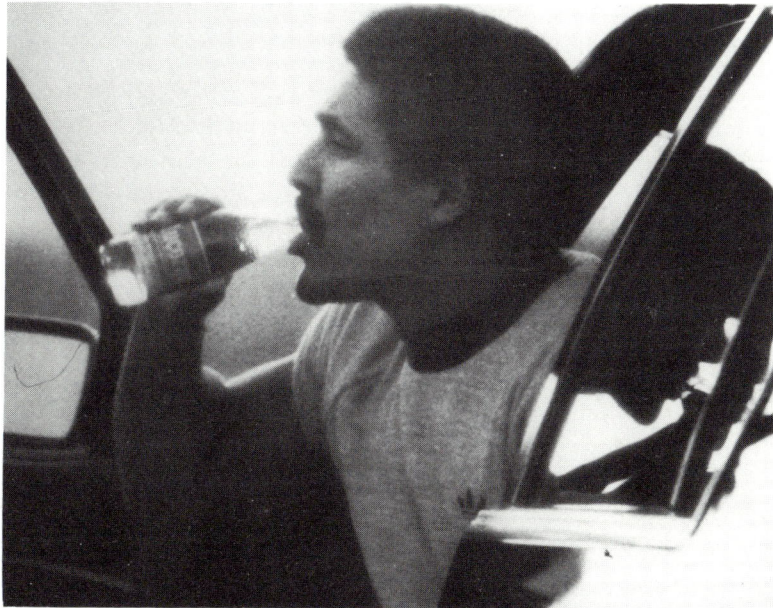

Lucozade Daley Thompson

The showing of the Daley commercials coincided with the largest sales increase Lucozade has had in the last decade.

The last word is left to the Beecham Foods Chairman, John Robb. He has described (*Financial Times*, 30 November 1983) how he 'trebled the annual advertising spend since 1977 and introduced the notion that Lucozade provides energy rather than just improved health. Sterling sales responded smartly more than doubling to between £25 and £30 million today.'

Conclusions

■ Old product development requires skilful balancing. The old consumer franchise is vital, while the new consumer franchise is the future blood of the brand.

■ This case history demonstrates how advertising can play the key role in revitalizing an established brand of great importance.

■ This is not just a case of one campaign being better than the previous one, but the development of more relevant advertising.

■ We also see priority being given to profit, reflected in a rise in consumer price. Nevertheless, a resilient brand and good repositioning can sustain sales volume.

■ Provided the signs are recognized early enough, the analysis done thoroughly and the correct action taken, a great product in temporary decline can be turned around successfully. But it does require both the will to do it, and the courage of your convictions to see it through.

13

Defending from strength: the *Sunday Express* challenged by the *Mail on Sunday*

Marketplace

The overall Sunday newspaper market has been in gentle decline for some years. Sunday newspapers are quite different from weekly newspapers: the reader looks for more variety within his Sunday paper than he would expect to find in his daily paper, for the Sunday newspaper is an important part of the weekend. He looks for a balance between news and entertainment, and the Sunday paper is lingered over and read in depth. This market has traditionally grouped itself into popular papers and up-market papers − with the exception of the *Sunday Express*, which has taken a position between these extremes.

The lack of competition in this middle sector was seen to be an opportunity by the *Mail on Sunday*, especially given the successful coexistence of the *Daily Mail* with the *Daily Express*. The *Sunday Express* was viewed as being vulnerable as it had not changed noticeably over the years; it was also thought, by certain media commentators, to have a relatively ageing consumer profile.

The *Daily Mail* had conversely been undergoing a renaissance against the *Daily Express*; and with many *Daily Mail* readers taking the *Sunday Express*, it was thought that it would be easy pickings for Associated Newspapers if they were to launch a seventh-day version of their successful daily contender against

Express Newspapers' 'ageing dinosaur'. One third of the *Daily Mail*'s readers read the *Sunday Express* and a quarter of *Sunday Express* readers read the *Daily Mail* — a group of some 750,000 purchasers — on the surface, an obvious potential target for the *Mail on Sunday*.

Media pundits on all sides of the industry forecasted a virtually unqualified success for the *Mail on Sunday*, with the predominant view being that its business success would be largely at the expense of the *Sunday Express*. Its objective of 1.25 million circulation was even thought by some to be an underestimate. Some forecasters predicted a possible 750,000 loss of sales for the *Sunday Express*.

How the Mailed fist will hit the Sunday Express

The publishers must anticipate most of this circulation coming from disaffected readers of the *Sunday Express* which should lose at least half a million circulation if the *Mail On Sunday* is to be successful.

I happen to believe that the Mail on Sunday will be a great success and that the Sunday Express will have to be altered if it is not to lose a major chunk of its readership to the new title.

The *Sunday Express* has most to fear, with its declining circulation and an ageing readership profile.

Young and Rubicam's media bulletin *Time and Space*, says that the *Mail on Sunday*, poses the greatest threat to the *Sunday Express*.

Sunday Express: the forecasters predicted disaster.

A newspaper loses money in two ways from a circulation drop. Not only is its cover price revenue directly affected, but its advertising revenue depends — though not directly — on having a reasonable size of readership to offer advertisers. Newspaper economics are complex: marketing spend to defend circulation has to be balanced to help both sources of revenue.

Advertising strategy

Importantly, we were in the position of being able to offer our client an independent appraisal of the size of the threat. We did so without the hysteria of the trade press, basing our estimates on analyses of the National Readership Survey and of our own Life Style research, plus some telephone interviews specifically about the forthcoming launch. In our analysis unit we also had a twenty-year history of newspaper circulations, with a study of how these had been affected by cover prices relative to those of other papers – a major determinant of sales.

The *Sunday Express*, like most papers, reacts to cover price, but not in the dramatic way of most products which many consumers see as easily substituted. This relatively low price elasticity was a clue to its resilience. In fact, in 1981, circulation rose despite two increases in cover price – from 20p to 22p and then 25p – in less than a year. The introduction of the colour magazine, adding value to the basic product, reinforced this underlying resilience.

The duplication of *Sunday Express* readership with readers of the *Daily Mail* is high. We found in our interviews that these people expressed an above-average interest in the forthcoming competitor.

We considered also our infrequent readers. Not all people are totally loyal to a Sunday newspaper in the sense that they read every issue. We felt that as many as a third of our readers were at least in the market for a new paper.

On closer inspection the reality of the position of the *Sunday Express* was not as insecure as many of its critics thought. The *Sunday Express* still offered the advertiser a readership of nearly eight million, with more AB readers than any other paper. Clearly the paper still had great strengths that were not fully appreciated, but perhaps the greatest of all was that the *Sunday Express* already had a strong franchise of almost three million circulation – the *Mail on Sunday* had to start from scratch and *win* its franchise.

In the end we made judgements, based on these and other facts. We assumed that the *Mail on Sunday* would print and sell their forecast 1,250,000 copies when sales settled down. Sales taken from the *Sunday Express* and the 'qualities' we expected to be in proportion to these newspapers' circulations, modified by duplication with the *Daily Mail*. The latter figure expressed our belief that the *Sunday Express* had an above-average proportion of its readership at risk.

In this way we arrived at our own estimate (Table 13.1) of the *Sunday Express's* probable circulation loss — on the assumption that there was no advertising against the attack.

Enlarging the market (extra paper, first paper)	250,000
From 'populars'	350,000
From Sunday Express	325,000
From 'qualities'	325,000

Although less than half as large as some estimates, a loss of 325,000 circulation still had to be guarded against, provided the cost of doing so was reasonable.

One thing that had been true in recent years of the *Sunday Express* was that it had received relatively little marketing support, and it was clear to both the client and the agency that considerable effort would have to be put into devising an effective strategy to optimize defences for the coming combat.

Public criticism of the *Sunday Express* often cited an apparent lack of change over time as one of its weaknesses. Hence the starting point of the *Sunday Express* strategy had to be the question: 'Given the launch of the first serious alternative into the middle market, should the *Sunday Express* undertake some kind of change or facelift?'. Industry speculation ranged from those envisaging no change at all, to those who hazarded a possible reformulation as a tabloid.

The first task was to determine the extent to which the paper was really strong. Had it enjoyed a three-million sale simply because there was no alternative? To answer this key question, after discussion with Express Group marketing executives, we mounted a number of qualitative and quantitative research studies to assess the real strengths of the paper.

The qualitative research exercise comprised twenty-four in-depth interviews amongst ABC1 regular readers of the *Sunday Express*. The sample was subdivided into some solus readers, some who also read a quality Sunday newspaper, some who also read a popular Sunday newspaper, and some who also read the *Daily Mail* during the week. Prior to this we had conducted four group discussions amongst *Sunday Express* readers in which we explored the strengths and weaknesses of the paper. The results gave us guidance on what sort of people our readers were and what aspects of the *Sunday Express* they enjoyed. This helped us to design the re-ordering of the newspaper.

In this qualitative work we experimentally reordered the normal sequence of *Sunday Express* features. When confronted with this irregular vision of their paper, *Sunday Express* readers had no hesitation in saying how much they preferred the original. The unchanging nature of the *Sunday Express* is not the weakness the pundits forecast, but instead is one of its greatest strengths! Consistent layout and regular features act as familiar landmarks and serve to nurture loyalty of readers to a paper they feel content and happy with.

This study supported the *Sunday Express* editor's view that there should be no radical change, but also revealed that the opportunity for minor, carefully planned evolution did exist. During the run-up to the launch of the *Mail on Sunday*, the traditional 'society' column was relocated from page two to give room for more hard news. Changes to typefaces were undertaken, and even the masthead was restyled – small but important changes carried out slowly and almost imperceptibly so as not to disrupt the crucial allegiance of the reader to his concept of the 'unchanging' *Sunday Express*.

A further finding of qualitative research, beyond the need to resist any pressure for major change, indicated that the readers' familiarity and long-standing loyalty to the paper, together with a history of little advertising support, had combined to diffuse their ability to explain exactly why they had chosen to read the *Sunday Express*. Further probing, however, produced ready answers – the strength of the regular features, such as John Junor's column and the Giles cartoon, plus the whole role of the paper as a valued part of the weekend. It became clear that an essential part of the strategy must be to remind readers of the value of these regular features.

If dramatic confirmation of the existing strengths of the paper was to be the key to retaining the *current* readers, what else could be brought to bear to attract *new* readership? There was never any doubt about the strategic importance of this task, as any mass-market newspaper must continually attract people if it is to replace the natural erosion of its readership over time.

Both the client and the agency believed that the best answer to this question lay in the competitive advantage that the *Sunday Express* would have, at the time of the launch of the *Mail on Sunday*, through the Colour Magazine. Launched in April 1981, this represented the ideal opportunity to attract new readers to the paper.

Therefore, soon after the launch of the *Sunday Express Magazine*, Leo Burnett and Express Newspapers jointly commissioned research involving 1000 telephone interviews to find what Sunday newspapers people were reading, what role Sunday newspapers fulfilled, and their views of their Sunday papers — for example, the importance of a colour magazine, of political stance, etc.

The findings from this research and our qualitative research showed that the launch of the magazine had had its problems. Readership figures for the magazine were below those for the paper itself. Opportunities thus existed to improve both the content and the appearance of the magazine. A particularly significant agency input to this improvement programme was the redesign of the front cover.

The strategic role of the magazine was developed through a series of features, each designed to run for several weeks, and organized to overlap so that a set of these mini 'part-works' would cover the whole launch period of the *Mail on Sunday*. Topics ranging from gardening to cookery were included, with pride of position being given to the serialization of Robert Lacey's book on the Princess of Wales. Editorial knowledge and judgement on which topics to select was considerably helped by guidance on items most likely to appeal to *Sunday Express* readers, derived from the agency's life style and qualitative research.

With the essence of the strategy now agreed, the next job was to develop advertising that dramatized the traditional strengths of the paper and at the same time optimized the appeal of the revamped magazine.

Advertising development

The first task was to find a campaign theme that really would capture the virtues of the paper and reinforce its value to the readers in a strong and positive way. This exercise brought us to 'The *Sunday Express* — it adds so much to Sunday' as the best exposition of what the paper represented. In order to take advantage of the magazine, this became 'The *Sunday Express* with Colour Magazine — it adds so much to Sunday'.

Using this as a base, our advertising went on to punch home those traditional strengths of the paper that made it so much part of the readers' Sunday — such as the depth of its sports coverage, the appeal of the regular columnists, the strength of its cartoonists, the correctness of its editorial stance. This thematic support of the paper was balanced with other advertisements designed to draw attention to the new-look magazine and its latest content.

As the launch of the *Mail on Sunday* grew nearer, the campaign was designed to develop a sharper edge, with posters that proclaimed the loss to readers should they give up their *Sunday Express*. 'Sunday without Giles — no laughing matter' and 'Sunday without the *Sunday Express* Magazine — colourless' were two of the poster advertisements which developed the 'Adds so much to Sunday' theme in the last few weeks before the competitor's launch.

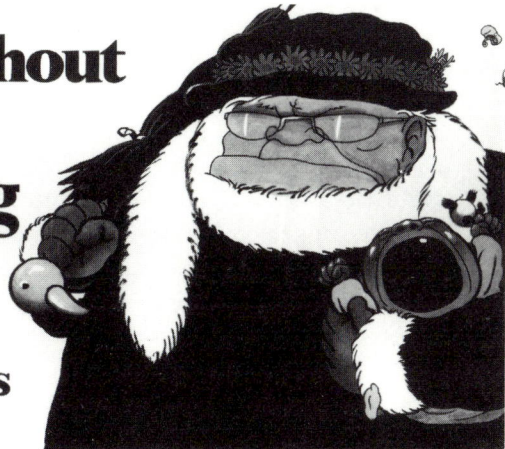

Sunday Express: 48-sheet poster

The first television treatments were made in time to pre-empt the pre-launch publicity of the *Mail* and majored on two important serialized features — Frederick Forsyth's new book in the paper, and Robert Lacey's *Princess* in the magazine. Later television work was designed to reinforce the identified traditional strengths of the paper, with some dramatization of special features in either paper or magazine.

Campaign

Media planning could take advantage of the fact that we knew in advance exactly when the *Mail on Sunday* would launch. Therefore we could set our own ideal timetable for the preparation of our defences, running through March and April, in advance of the 1 May launch date of the competitor.

The substantial use of national forty-eight sheet posters was the first step in our pre-emptive strategy. Posters were chosen because of their ability to offer highly visible and continuous presence throughout the run-up period. They provided the medium for the establishment of the basic theme and regular, sometimes fortnightly, copy changes kept the campaign alive and intrusive.

The traditional strengths of the paper and virtues of the colour magazine now established with posters, the campaign moved into television on the weekend before the launch of the *Mail on Sunday*. We had decided that, rather than compete with the massive advertising that Associated Newspapers would throw behind their new venture on its eve of launch, the media timing for the *Sunday Express* would continue to precede theirs. Our money was spent the previous weekend to publicize the two major serials in paper and magazine, with the intention that, once hooked by the appeal of the features, the readers' loyalty would be reinforced over this crucial period.

The *Mail on Sunday* appeared with the expected massive publicity, but to a mixed reception from the media. Early figures suggested that the *Sunday Express* strategy was working, for following the appearance of the *Mail on Sunday* during the first week of May, the overall May sales figures for the *Sunday Express* showed a loss of only 37,000 compared with April, and this during a period when the publicity for the *Mail on Sunday* was at its height. Remember that some pundits had forecast a drop of up to 750,000, and our own studies had suggested that 325,000 copies were at risk.

Contrary to the conventional wisdom of not supporting newspapers during the summer, the decision was taken to press home the successful counter to the launch of the *Mail on Sunday* by advertising through the summer. A policy of efficiently directing funds against key regions, where the appeal of the *Mail on Sunday* would be strongest, was followed from June to September using advertising which continued to remind the reader of the key strengths of the paper and its magazine, as well as dramatizing the occasional special feature in either paper or colour supplement. An additional tactic sustained throughout the campaign was a regular full page advertisement in each Saturday's *Daily Express* which set out to stimulate interest in the specifics of the following day's paper.

By late summer the *Mail on Sunday* sales were clearly disappointing to Associated Newspapers, resulting in a widely publicized editorial bloodbath and a decision to rush out an unscheduled relaunch in late October. This relaunch augmented the revised paper with a new colour magazine.

Armed with the knowledge of this intended relaunch, the *Sunday Express* prepared the second phase of its campaign. The decision was to adopt the same successful strategy used at the time of the original launch. We would use posters and television and pre-empt the *Mail on Sunday* with a strong serialized feature that would carry through their launch period. The subject chosen on this occasion was a new collection of formal and informal royal photographs taken by Patrick Lichfield.

Evaluation

Up to October 1982, the policies followed by the *Sunday Express* were to make only minor changes to format and to use our advertising to reinforce reader loyalty. Table 13.2 shows the result.

| | Circulation | | Change |
	April 82 (000)	October 82 (000)	October on April (per cent)
Sunday Express	2940	2815	−4.3
Sunday Mirror	3741	3577	−4.4
Sunday People	3533	3418	−3.3
News of the World	4366	4175	−4.4
Sunday Times	1303	1279	−1.8
Sunday Telegraph	866	791	−8.7
Observer	867	808	−6.8
Mail on Sunday		1018	

Table 13.2

The *Sunday Express* fared no worse than any popular Sunday newspaper — and better than two of the 'qualities'. The

163

circulation loss was only 125,000. The *Sunday Telegraph* was the largest percentage loser, suggesting that the readers of that paper were not particularly loyal, or were sufficiently dissatisfied with their paper to make the change to the *Mail on Sunday*.

Advertising had convincingly shown that it could help retain the overwhelming majority of our circulation.

Postscript

Since the end of this case history the *Mail on Sunday* has been spending considerable sums to buy a position in the marketplace – not only on its content, now including a magazine, but on promotion. Up to June 1983 a further 1600 rating points on television supported the paper.

It does not make commercial sense for the *Sunday Express* to match this sort of expenditure. In fact, in the same period we have had less than 100 ratings and no posters. The *Sunday Express* is in a sound business position as a result. Its circulation drop to June 1983 (370,000 from April 1982) is close to what we predicted would be the case without advertising, but is noticeably less than many had predicted.

Conclusions

■ The tremendous latent strength of the *Sunday Express*, identified and successfully harnessed by Express Newspapers and Leo Burnett in the months before the appearance of the *Mail on Sunday*, produced a firm and effective rebuff to Associated Newspapers' attempt to seize the *Sunday Express* franchise.

■ Two decisions turned out to be critical. First, in the case of the *Sunday Express*, radical editorial change would have been suicidal, though there were many who urged it at the time. The continuity and unchanging image of the paper was a fundamental strength.

Second, loyalty to the paper was reinforced by advertising which was pre-emptive in timing and reassuring about features we knew were treasured. It was this strengthening of reader loyalty which held circulation against the challenge from the *Mail on Sunday*.

■ More generally, a lesson is that change of a product for change's sake is not essential. Once we are sure that the user is generally satisfied − and we have to approach this question sceptically and independently − then the product need not be artificially reformulated. It is of crucial importance to strategy to work hard to isolate and understand the existing strengths of a product or service.

■ Advertising that confirms behaviour and defends, can be as useful as advertising that changes behaviour and attacks. The *Sunday Express* lost some sales. We regard the containment of this loss as a success, and so does our client.

14

Kotex Simplicity Towels: the effect of the unexpected

Marketplace

It might be supposed that advertising for sanitary protection would be of high interest to women — and that they would be eager to seek out details of good products which are of particular benefit at this time of the month.

The reverse is in fact the case. The market, whilst changing more rapidly than ever nowadays, remains extremely conservative. There are persistent negative attitudes toward discussion of the problem in any public forum, including advertising.

Most women would prefer to read about other things in the advertisements (as opposed to the editorial) in their magazines. They are generally aware of the range of products available, but their awareness of advertising is extremely low.

Evidence of this resistance and disinterest is available from various sources. First, it is a consistent finding in group discussions conducted on behalf of Kimberly-Clark by different researchers on different projects. Women have considerable difficulty in spontaneously recalling sanitary protection advertisements.

Second, on a quantified level, advertising tracking studies demonstrate that, to achieve a score of 10 per cent spontaneous awareness, even on an extremely well-established towel brand, is a major achievement.

Third, from an independent perspective, IPC provide evaluative assessment work conducted on sanitary protection and other advertisements. This clearly demonstrates that,when compared with average scores derived from assessment of other female interest product fields, sanitary protection advertising generally suffers from low recall, low involvement and low brand identification.

It is clear from these sources that a basic disinclination to read advertisements on the subject is further compounded by the fact that any press advertisement has to compete for attention in magazines which are crowded with competition. In 1981 no less than sixteen brands packed nearly £5 million worth of expenditure into the medium. It is arguable that this inclines the reader even further to avoid the onslaught of advertising on the topic.

But in planning Simplicity Towels advertising we knew from a separate Leo Burnett analysis of the factors influencing sales that, given a situation where relative price did not over-influence the other variables, advertising is capable of making a positive contribution to the maintenance or growth of a brand.

Getting through to the consumer is a particularly difficult advertising task in this market – though advertising also 'worked' in other measurable ways.

As a result, all our strategic thinking in 1982 was placed in the context of the question: 'How can we improve our advertising visibility in order to make the budgets work harder?'.

It was a particularly pertinent time to consider this problem since the market was becoming increasingly competitive. Simplicity Towels was the brand leader, and in a position of traditional strength. It could nevertheless be eroded by the launch of new contenders, especially a new generation of slim sanitary towels.

Recourse to television, an obvious and traditional way to increase awareness, was denied us since the test conducted by the IBA resulted in some complaints about invasion of women's privacy. On such a sensitive topic contractors and manufacturers alike agreed not to pursue further the use of that medium.

Posters are in theory available, but it is probable that their very 'public' nature makes them unacceptable.

All the members of the Leo Burnett team – client service, planning, media and creative – set out, therefore, to pursue every means of increasing advertising visibility.

Such an achievement would be an end in itself, but it was our belief that a successful advertising solution would make a positive contribution to sales.

Advertising strategy

The most important strategic decision we took was on media — not *what* we would say in our communication, which was already agreed, but *where* we would say it.

Women's press was at the time virtually the sole medium for sanitary protection advertising. On the surface it is the ideal medium for advertising of this nature.

It talks to women in a personal environment, through their own reading matter. It offers the impact of colour, a major creative benefit. It is possible to be very precise about the type of women we are addressing through the different magazines. A strong schedule of magazines is capable of reaching a very high national coverage of the target market.

Before any more drastic steps were considered we asked ourselves some tough questions on our women's press work. Were our advertisements strong enough, both strategically and executionally? Was our space buying giving us the maximum possible awareness for the money?

We were helped by a qualitative research programme which considered strategic and executional options for press advertising. In pursuit of stand-out we adopted drawings as opposed to photographic illustrations, and we experimented with unconventional space sizes.

The more we considered the problem overall, however, the more we decided that the expected route, however optimized, would not achieve the kind of visibilty leap we were looking for.

We had to look for the unexpected. This, whatever the theoretical merits of women's press, we adjudged meant a change of direction — a method of surprising the consumer by sending a message in an unexpected way.

With television and posters ruled out, the other methods of attack were national press and commercial radio.

National press, by its newsy nature, can make an important contribution to announcing the launch of a new product. It is valuable in this market where the advertising task is often promotional — for example, communicating special offers or providing coupons to the consumer. But it was rapidly apparent to us that its black and white nature seriously limited its ability to carry advertising that reflected the correct tonal values for our brand, Simplicity Towels.

Clearly the colour element of women's magazines was a vital element in the projection of the right personality for the brand. Newspapers could not compare in this regard. They could provide visibility – but visibility without colour, stripped of its emotional content.

Commercial radio, on the other hand, offered the important tonal contributions of music and voice. Deeper consideration and assessment of the nature of this medium and of its relationship with its audience revealed four further important reasons for cementing a decision to change media direction to radio. This would not be total, but an overlay on our press work, designed to uplift the visibility (or is it audibility?) of our brand.

First, since there are times in the day when many women are alone listening to radio, it can be (like press) a selective and personal medium, offering effectively a one-to-one communication.

Second, the listening audience is young – particularly important when any threat to Simplicity Towels could come from younger women tempted to try 'younger' products.

Third, radio is a relatively young medium; and we believed the very fact that the name Simplicity was heard on radio would 'update' its image to some degree.

Fourth, the medium is very flexible. Regions of the country (even towns) can be bought separately, making it easy to test an idea before spending large sums of money on a national basis. And commercials can be designed to be thematic, selling the brand, or tactical, incorporating information about special offers and deals.

Over and above this, radio is a new and exciting medium to work with creatively. It gave our creative people the welcome chance of developing work in non-traditional territory. We all realized it was a unique (and taxing) opportunity to strike a successful balance between discretion and excitement.

Advertising development

Having taken the first key decision, to move into a medium

where the consumers would not normally expect us to be, we embarked on the task of creating the unexpected. We wanted to make a specifically aural contribution to enhanced visibility for the brand.

Extreme care had to be exercised here on two dimensions. First, we had to have exciting creative work that nevertheless did not break the bounds of propriety in what is, inevitably, a delicate area for advertising.

Second, in line with the nature of the medium and the target audience, we needed work that was young, modern and innovative but without being at odds with the traditional and reassuring virtues of an established brand-leader.

Qualitative research work was employed to investigate the validity of the current advertising proposition for the brand. This confirmed the correctness of our positioning. There was no need to change our proposition radically in the way we had redirected our media choice.

The basis of the creative brief was to keep all work on the same time-honoured strategy, positioning Simplicity Towels as 'the safest full-size press-on towel'. We expressed that proposition by situations in which women have no concern about staying out longer than planned, having to cope with an unexpected delay, because they know they can rely on Simplicity Towels to 'stay the course'.

We called the existing creative theme 'the extended day'. Our creatives had had no difficulty in illustrating this theme in press — for example, when a woman and her family decide to stay longer on a picnic, or a change in the weather means a delay somewhere on a day out.

Several initial radio approaches, all dramatizing the agreed strategy in different ways, were professionally recorded as advertisements. All were carefully tested among groups of the target audience. No clear winner emerged, but this was a valuable exercise because very clear guidelines for the development of successful work were apparent. Encouragingly the women interviewed were not only of the opinion that local radio was a totally acceptable advertising medium, but also that none of our initial test executions was offensive, embarassing or in any way anxiety-provoking.

From this exploratory exercise we learned about the acceptable tones of advertising — those which suited our target — and the kinds of women it was best for us to portray.

With the encouragement of consumer enthusiasm we created a campaign. The final commercials were certainly unexpected. So much so that, in a field not known for innovation, we have collected several major creative awards.

We found ourselves on radio with a campaign involving rock and disco – not exactly where we expected to be and, thankfully in a positive way, not where the consumer expected us to be either.

The three situations 'Fairground', 'Day Tripper' and 'Disco' featured lyrics describing days out where unexpected delays meant staying longer, but without any concern – right on the mainstream Simplicity Towels strategy.

An infectious tune coupled with strong, modern and relevant lyrics designed for female singers added up to noticeable and, importantly, enjoyable radio advertising (Figure 14.1).

RADIO SCRIPT FROM LEO BURNETT LIMITED

Client:	KIMBERLY-CLARK	Script No:	
Product:	SIMPLICITY TOWELS	Date:	28TH AUGUST 1981
Length:	40 SECONDS	Creative Group:	CW

DISCO

Girl singing:

I had a t.t.t.t.tremendous time.
I left the office early. I was feelin' fine.
We tried a disco that was new.
I wore my favourite gold and blue.
I danced all night without a care.
I met a chap so debonnaire!
And when they played the final track--

    He said.... How about a Pizza?

Girl singing:

So in a flash we're sitting in this pizza place.
And I'm quite glad the others couldn't stand the pace.
And just imagine my delight,
he asked me out again tonight.
I had a t.t.t.t.tremendous time.

Female VO:

I can enjoy a day like that any day of the month,
because I use those Simplicity Press-on towels.

They're so safe, I never have a moment's worry.

Kotex Simplicity. There's simply nothing safer.

Figure 14.1 Radio script for Simplicity Towels advertisement

The final versions of this creative idea were also carefully researched among a large sample of the target audience.

One of the commercials in the campaign was placed in a reel of existing radio commercials of interest to female listeners and played in a test situation. Later, informants filled in a self-completion questionnaire. Responses were elicited after both first and second hearings of the commercial.

The results were very encouraging. Satisfactory proportions of the target recalled the main message and the brand; enough agreed that the commercial was 'talking to someone like me'.

Nearly half spontaneously described the commercial as lively, bouncy and catchy − particularly impressive scores in a product field where so many refuse to admit they look or listen.

Campaign

The campaign was planned to cover a nine-month period, with a proviso that the second and third bursts would proceed only if the first and longest burst of advertising produced measurable improvements. The changes were looked for in terms of increased awareness of advertising and an even more positive brand image.

It was decided to test the new radio campaign on quite a large scale. We selected the London, Midlands and Scotland areas. This selection was carefully considered, and based on two factors:

■ the strength of the brand − in sales and distribution

■ the level of potential radio coverage achievable in the areas.

In total, fifteen radio stations participated in the test in these areas.

We did not expect significant movements in terms of awareness of Simplicity Towels itself, since brand awareness was already high. We were looking for positive sales move-

Simplicity: magazine advertising on the same strategy as the radio campaign

ment, but we did not expect sudden and massive upswings. We were looking for positive shifts on certain dimensions that would encourage us to invest further in radio over a longer period and on a wider scale.

The first burst of radio was in Autumn 1981 when women's press advertisements were also appearing. The construction of the radio schedule was planned in considerable detail. ITCA regulations prevented us from using 'breakfast' radio times (Monday to Friday, 7—9 a.m.) and obviously children's programmes. Additionally we decided to avoid times of day when large numbers of children might be listening (for example, weekday lunchtimes and late afternoons).

We had already concluded we should place the bulk of the airtime when we believed women were actually more likely to be listening alone — Monday to Friday mornings (9—12 a.m.) and afternoons (2—4 p.m.).

Finally, we boosted the campaign with additional spots before 7 a.m. and after 11 p.m., when product usage is particularly relevant.

The final schedule was a careful balance between legal constraints, product usage and listening behaviour. It also gave satisfactory levels of coverage and frequency.

A final decision was to transmit the 'Disco' version of the campaign idea at times when younger listeners would be tuned in.

Evaluation

A programme of four research surveys, one before and three at different stages during the campaign, was designed to track the effect of advertising on the target audience (women 16—54 who purchase and use press-on sanitary towels), primarily in terms of changes in awareness and attitudes to the brand.

The sample was drawn from the catchment areas of the three selected **ILR** regions, with a control sample selected from the catchment areas of ILR stations which were not included in the schedule.

In-home interviews were carried out. The quotas were set on age, social grade and working status to ensure a nationally representative sample of press-on towel users. The samples were sufficiently large for us to examine not only total movements in the radio test area, but also changes in the sub-sample of ILR listeners.

Given the importance of the radio advertising test to both Simplicity Towels in particular, and to Kotex feminine products in general, a series of action standards were set prior to the test. These included key advertising and brand noticeability measures, and specified the level of increase necessary to achieve a statistically significant result at the 95 per cent confidence level.

Even more gratifying, analysis of sales data reported from the Nielsen audit of sales in grocery and chemist outlets showed significant upward shifts in Simplicity Towels sales compared with the same periods in the previous year when radio was not used. When the test areas were compared with the control areas, sales where radio was used were higher.

Conclusions

■ A radio campaign can considerably improve the impact of the brand's advertising compared with a press schedule on its own.

■ A comprehensive research programme provided us with more general information on the impact of different weights and durations of radio advertising.

■ Significant increases in the proportions who had seen or heard any advertising for Kotex Simplicity Towels demonstrated that radio advertising is capable of reaching an additional section of the brand's target, not merely duplicating press advertising.

■ Even in a conservative market there are significant rewards available to those who take the unexpected route, both in choice of media and style of advertising. We should never be satisfied with doing things the traditional way.

15

Perrier: building a market and holding the share

Marketplace

The identification of a new market opportunity is the classical introduction to a successful case study. But whilst there are many examples where this has led to entrepreneurial success, history is littered with the tombstones of those initial pioneers who have been overwhelmed by the marketing muscle of larger companies, who have subsequently entered and dominated the market.

The sales growth of Perrier bottled mineral water in the UK is a striking and heartening example to those who still believe that success can be achieved, not just at launch, but continuously. It can be self-financed. Great creativity does not always require enormous resources. Advertising has a large role to play by establishing the strong brand image essential to resist competition.

Long before the introduction of Perrier into the UK, the seeds of opportunity had been sown early this century in the Nîmes area of France by Sir John Harmsworth of the famous newspaper family. Having been introduced to the local phenomena of deep bubbling springs by a local, Dr Perrier, he foresaw the potential for marketing the natural sparkling waters and adopted the now famous club-shaped bottle. He was selling 19 million bottles a year at his death in 1933.

The platform for wider growth was already emerging with exports accounting for around 50 per cent of this total business. These were being directed to important business and social centres, such as New York and London, where Perrier was already becoming part of a discerning life style.

A major impetus to continuing business expansion was the purchase of the spring, at the end of the Second World War, by Monsieur Gustave Leven, who is still the leading shareholder in Source Perrier — now the world's leading producer of sparkling mineral water, with sales in 119 countries.

In the UK, the decision by Aqualac Spring Waters Ltd, the UK subsidiary of Perrier, to introduce the one-litre sized bottle into supermarkets in 1974, proved to be a significant development. At that time the total bottled mineral water market was very small. Perrier sales were a mere 50,000 cases, all in the split-sized bottle.

Consumer experience of the product was generally limited to continental trips and holidays. This had generated no clear product image other than a vague belief that it was a minor, specialist and mildly eccentric product within the vast soft-drinks market.

In order to obtain the support of the retail trade for the new, more ambitious Perrier marketing programme, it was essential to develop a total promotional campaign reflecting a distinct brand personality very much stronger than its actual physical presence in the marketplace.

Advertising strategy

The overall advertising objective was therefore very clear, but hardly unique to Perrier. Because water is a basic necessity of life it is hardly surprising that marketeers since the year dot have spent vast sums on developing and promoting variations of the original basic product, with many and exciting embellishments.

Some of these product developments have been physically and technically significant — few, for example, would argue that wine is different from, if not better than, water. Some, as with proprietary whiskies, are mainly psychological (who can really tell the brand?). Others, such as Perrier, have been a mixture of both.

In addition to the appealing visual and drinking characteristics of the clear sparkling liquid, and the unique bottle, there were already signs of the type of brand personality that would be appropriate for a relevant target market.

The localized export markets, both in the UK and elsewhere,

not only indicated the higher social profile of existing drinkers, but strongly suggested that these consumers would be responsive to communication which recognized their self-flattering perceptions of themselves. We believed the target was potentially receptive of products which are associated with 'sophisticated' life styles.

The advertising strategy for Perrier was therefore to enhance the distinctive bottle and sparkling contents with a brand personality which reinforced perceptions of both consumers and the product as members of an exclusive club.

Advertising objective

In terms of creative execution, the Perrier campaign demonstrates a flexible response to the emergence of a Perrier personality. Within a consistently applied strategy, we have developed those attributes which work hardest in building the image of the brand.

From the mid-1970s, the unique visual elements of the product led us to a strong graphic treatment. With the need to support varying levels of local distribution, posters were the ideal media choice.

The first campaign concentrated on creating better brand awareness and majored on the unique bottle and label design. But by 1977, following a rush of competitive entrants into the market, this was extended to emphasize the French heritage of Perrier. This was continued in 1978 by building on the expanding penetration base with suggestions for wider product usage. The ensuing versatility campaign featured the brand as a table water, a mixer and just on its own as a great refreshing drink.

So by 1978 the basic framework of the Perrier campaign had been constructed.

The business was successfully expanding. Advertising awards were being won and, significantly, creative people were contesting to out-perform their colleagues. However, there remained a major concern that, although the advertising was both effective and on strategy, the emphasis was perhaps too ephemeral and dependent on tone.

With the number of competitors continuing to increase, there was a fundamental need for a long-term property which could

Picasseau.

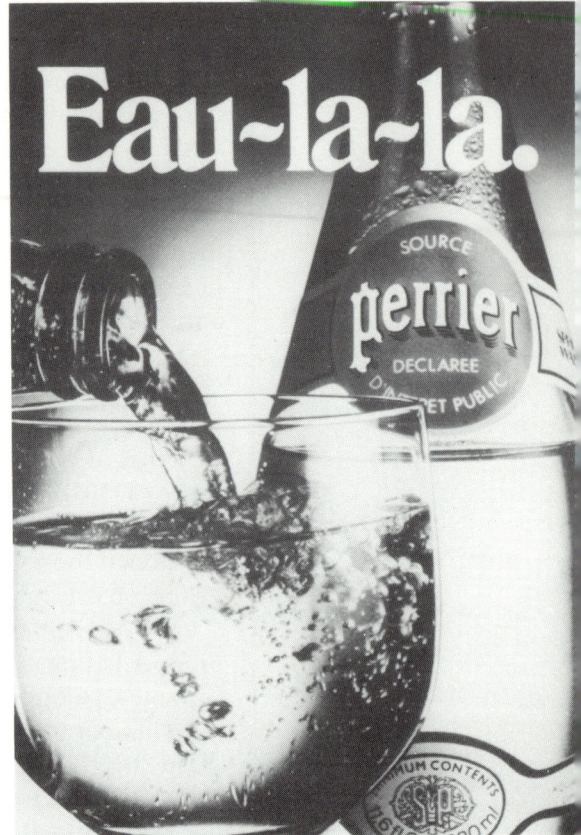

Eau-la-la.

maintain the distinct identity of this brand and provide a strong link between all aspects of the promotional programme.

The solution was already available in the 1978 campaign with the 'Eau la la' execution, and the 'Eau' theme was developed as the creative platform for all subsequent poster advertising.

'Eau' provided a shorthand way of saying unique, distinctive, French and fun. It produced an advertising campaign which maintained a unique and confident stance for the brand. More significantly, the use of the puns not only gave pleasure, but flattered the understanding of the Perrier drinker and endorsed their self-perceived exclusivity. Julian Bowes, the chief executive of Aqualac (Spring Waters) said the consumer had had an 'intellectual love affair' with the advertising.

In addition to providing the platform for a continuing series of executions which generally extended the awareness and appeal of the campaign, the 'Eau' theme enabled more specific tactical communication objectives to be tackled in the same direct and simple style. For example, 'N'eau Calories' highlights the slimming aspects of Perrier, 'Bubbles made by nature' talks health and 'Eau la la' is celebratory. This was achieved with no copy explanation other than the headline — it allowed visual concentration on the physical attributes of the brand, and this has been one of the greatest creative strengths.

Campaign

Since the initial advertising in the mid-1970s, the main medium for the Perrier campaign has been posters. In more recent years we have introduced other media, but these have all supported the outdoor activity.

Across the total period, advertising expenditure has been modest, being closely related to planned business targets. In the five years 1976–80 Perrier's cumulative advertising spend of £650,000 represented a very small proportion of total advertising in just the minerals sector of the soft-drinks market.

It has therefore been necessary to select both the detailed location and nature of media activity with precision. Not only has the region of advertising been generally limited to south-east England, but, within this, sites have been carefully chosen in two ways. First, ACORN data guided us to the most valuable parts of the country. Second, within these we linked key outlets with the travelling routes of the customers they serve. The limited budget resulted in the use of smaller poster sizes, and the campaign has primarily consisted of four- and sixteen-sheet treatments. These were initially concentrated in Adshel and railway locations, but have gradually extended to cover more widely based routes.

The main media activity was supported by parallel development of the campaign idea in the trade press and in-store merchandising material. The posters were adapted in mini-poster format as a key element in the sales-force distribution and business development programme.

Evaluation

In creative recognition and awards our campaign has proved

very satisfying. More to the point, volume sales since the effective launch date in 1974 rose consistently to achieve a tenfold increase by 1982 (Table 15.1).

Year	Index (1975 = 100)	Change(per cent)
1976	159	+59
1977	204	+28
1978	310	+52
1979	514	+65
1980	674	+31
1981	878	+30
1982	1075	+22

Table 15.1
Index of Perrier bottled mineral water sales

This dynamic sales performance is particularly significant in the overall market for bottled mineral water, for two main reasons. First, the initial growth up to 1978 effectively created a market from nothing without the added impetus of other branded activity. Second, ever since the entry of a multitude of competing products, totalling well over a hundred by 1982, the year-on-year sales growth has still continued. The market has risen to 40 million bottles, and now accounts for around £22 million of consumers' expenditure. The overall strength of the brand is underlined by its dominant 70 per cent share of the sparkling water category, which remains by far the most popular sector in spite of many competitive efforts to segment the market with still-water products.

The contribution made by Perrier in building the market is clearly indicated by the geographical development and distribution of sales across the UK. The part of south-east England covering some 35 per cent of the population which coincides with the location of the Perrier campaign, accounts for 60 per cent of total bottled mineral water sales. Furthermore, whilst this area has attracted the bulk of competitive entry and activity, Perrier sales distribution and share remains higher than elsewhere.

The link between the exposure and impact of the advertising campaign with consumer buying habits is extremely clear from demographic patterns. Over half of Perrier volume is purchased by AB households, with regular buyers accounting for an unusually high 50 per cent of overall sales – thus fully justifying the consistent application of the original strategy to concentrate both media and message on a selected minority consumer group.

In terms of further potential, the penetration and frequency of purchasing in relation to the total soft-drinks market suggests that considerable growth opportunities still exist. As the consumer base widens and branding, rather than educating attitudes, becomes a higher priority, Perrier is strongly placed to use its favourable image to keep its dominant position in the market.

It is always hard to change a winning campaign, but we judge that now the wider market requires more direct help in making its choice. The advertising we are currently running is different − but we hope will be no less successful.

Conclusions

■ Perrier has always financed its advertising out of the growth it has produced. Far from being an expense, advertising is seen correctly as a profit-maker.

■ It is important to recognize success once you have achieved it − not just acclaim but also sales-effectiveness.

■ It is also important to be ready to recognize a changed situation and to be brave enough to change strategy accordingly.

16

Launching the Austin Metro

Marketplace

The 1970s is widely recognized as the decade in which the British car industry suffered from industrial and economic problems of such magnitude that its continued existence was in doubt.

The introduction of imported small hatchback cars added considerably to the problems facing British Leyland, by significantly and increasingly eroding sales of the Mini, its most successful and highest selling vehicle.

The impact on British Leyland's share of the small-car sector (that is, 1.0 to 1.3 litre engines) was dramatic − its share fell from 50 per cent in 1973 to 30 per cent in 1979. Although the actual sales decline was cushioned by the growing popularity of small cars, this further highlighted the declining presence of British Leyland on the road; and total company share halved (50 per cent down to 25 per cent) in the five years to 1979.

Hence the task of the Metro, British Leyland's entry into the small hatchback arena, was formidable:

■ It was a late entry into the market.

■ The car itself, while a very fine machine and one demonstrably superior to the competition on a number of key features, was evolutionary, rather than revolutionary as the Mini had been. It risked the gibe that it was the last car of the 1970s rather than the first of the 1980s.

■ It had to overcome great public scepticism about British Leyland. The publicly stated strategy for the revival of the company was to be product-led. The Metro was the first of these new products. If it failed then it was probable that British Leyland would also fail.

Advertising strategy

Positioning of the Metro in relation to the Mini

The initial brief to Leo Burnett was based on the traditional and logical premise that the new car would eventually replace the existing model: the Mini would be phased out. It was therefore considered desirable to get maximum value from the Mini's high awareness and past popularity by closely associating both cars; and this was to be achieved by calling the new car the 'Mini-Metro', with equal emphasis on both elements.

However, the agency's examination of research into the buyers of Minis and of small hatchbacks revealed that these were two very discrete market segments – the two sorts of vehicle fulfil very different purposes.

The role of the Mini was essentially defined by the personality of the car (small, cheeky, nippy, highly manoeuvrable, economical, youthful, fun to drive) and by the needs of the owner for personal transport. Hence the owners tend to be young, single or without children, unisex, urban – wanting to express themselves through the car's character.

The small hatchback, on the other hand, fulfils another, more mundane, role of offering credible, economic family motoring. Hence the hatchback is bought by married men looking for a versatile car offering luggage-carrying capacity for the family, comfortable on long distances as well as for urban driving, and with the size and flexibility to cope with a wide variety of demands.

These requirements were very different from those of the Mini buyer, and Metro fulfilled them extremely well.

We recommended a change to British Leyland, and the following strategic decisions were agreed:

■   to position the Metro single-mindedly against the small hatchback market

■   to retain the Mini range to cater for its own considerable and enduring demand

■   in particular to move Metro away from Mini by (a) always referring to the car as 'Metro', not 'Mini-Metro', and (b) encouraging the use of this name in pre-launch editorial and PR (while the Mini-Metro badging had to be retained for legal reasons, we played down the word 'Mini' as far as possible).

Competitive positioning of the Metro against other small hatchbacks

The timing of the Metro's entry into the market meant that purchasers would need to be obtained from those who would otherwise have bought competitive hatchbacks – that is, conquest purchases.

Our examination of research into the motivations for the selection and purchase of new cars underlined that there were both rational and emotional judgements on which decisions were based. The very specific model attributes which, in the main, could be demonstrated, compared and given priorities in a logical manner, needed to be presented within an overall proposition which emotionally satisfied the personality requirements of the buyer.

A series of group discussions amongst recent hatchback buyers showed that the Metro was considered to be outstanding on several of the most important attributes for that type of car (Table 16.1). This was quite conclusive evidence of the strength of the rational benefits of the Metro.

Attribute (in order of ranking)	Metro outstanding
Economy (particularly fuel economy)	x
Interior/boot space	x
Exterior style	x
Price/value for money	x
Reputation	
Performance	
Manœuvrability	
Service costs	x
Nationality	x

Table 16.1
Criteria important to selection of small hatchback car

We followed up with a second series of group discussions to establish the emotional hook which would make the overall proposition most effective. These were conducted amongst a range of respondents representing hatchback owners, Mini owners and other BL car owners.

In response to exposure to both the car and different advertising concepts, there was clear reassurance that there would be ready acceptance of the rational benefits. There were also strong indications of the priorities which should be attached to the roles of these functional attributes – outstanding fuel economy (60 miles per gallon), running economy (12,000 miles between services), and the versatility of interior space (unique seat flexibility).

WITH 12,000 MILES BETWEEN SERVICES, METRO RULES THE BAYS.

METRO

AUSTIN

Metro poster

Metro TV commercial: Britian has been invaded...

Now we have the means to fight back

The new Metro is so aerodynamic

...12,000 miles or one full year between services

A British car...

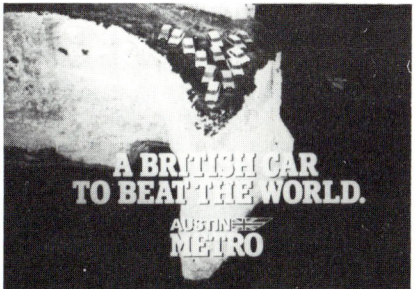

...to beat the world

Most importantly, the research also provided clear guidance on the emotional hook. It identified an emotional desire to buy British and, in particular, a strong undercurrent of positive feeling for British Leyland: people very much wanted to see BL get it right again, and were clearly willing to support the company if it did.

But whereas in the past people would automatically buy British on the assumption that they were getting a superior product, in 1980 this was no longer the case. Much as they wanted to, they simply did not believe they would get a superior product, especially from British Leyland. So, while the product was right, the treatment was critical. Disbelief had to be overcome.

Of the various concepts shown, a 'British car to beat the world', treated in an up-beat, modern, confident way and *supported by the right product and the right rational benefits*, struck exactly the required note of pride in heritage and of British success for a change. It had the capacity to overcome the underlying disbelief. Internal worries that we might be going over the top were dispelled by this research.

Advertising development

Against the agreed theme, a full package of launch advertising was developed and researched amongst key hatchback and British Leyland motorists. This contained television, press and outdoor treatments. It was confirmed as delivering a credible overall proposition within which key rational benefits were clearly communicated.

In addition, the results gave considerable executional guidelines, particularly with the television script, where the note to be struck was one of confidence in the future of a great British car. The patriotic appeal had to be firmly based in the present, and not retreat too far into a jingoistic past.

The campaign that evolved from this was developed into both a package of media advertising and dealer showroom support material.

Campaign

The importance and magnitude of the new car's introduction

required that the Metro launch should achieve immediate recognition as the most significant motoring event for several years. Whilst this was to be achieved by effective coordination of the total package of PR, editorial, showroom and dealer activity with the basic consumer campaign, the specific tasks for media advertising were considerable.

The highly fragmented and dynamic nature of the market-place meant that competitive activity would be at a very high level. Total television, press and outdoor advertising expenditure on cars was approaching £100 million a year. Nearly £20 million was spent on television and press in the fourth quarter of 1980, when the Metro was launched. Quite clearly the objective was to dominate major media, by providing a weight and range of message exposure as quickly as possible.

The media launch in October 1980 was spearheaded by a combination of sixty-second television commercials running for two weeks, supported by double-page press advertisements in national newspapers and more specialist publications, together with the highly relevant use of key local papers extending the emotional appeal to the critical group of BL employees. Large posters (forty-eight sheets) continued the campaign for the next two months to the end of the year.

This highly concentrated plan enabled the Metro to achieve around 20 per cent of car advertising during its launch month, and some 10 per cent in the whole quarter.

Evaluation

The launch of the Metro was outstandingly successful.

In addition to the major competitive presence achieved in media advertising, the general and specialist press editorial coverages and receptions were excellent.

After the first few weeks of media advertising, recall of the campaign as measured by the British Leyland Continuous Advertising Tracking Study was at an unparalleled high level − both TV (63 per cent) and press (58 per cent) achieving best-ever recall scores amongst cars. Perhaps even more impressive was the fact that this initial campaign impact was still sufficient to achieve the highest recall ratings (58 per cent TV and 55 per cent press) at the beginning of February, even though no further advertising had taken place. Even by the end of March, recall remained over 40 per cent without additional support.

The quality of this awareness was favourably high. Information collected in the same tracking study in early February established that the Metro was already the second most desired car in the small-car sector, with particularly good ratings on key rational criteria (Table 16.2).

	Metro (per cent)	Highest (per cent)
Car you would like to own	38	41
Good value for money	31	38
Costs less to maintain	24	37
Plenty of room inside	31	38

Table 16.2
Small car preferences
(Feb.81)

	Austin	Morris	Highest
Would seriously consider buying (per cent)	18	13	47

Table 16.3
Small — upper medium
manufacturer preferences
(Feb 81)

These scores were particularly impressive compared with the overall view towards British Leyland cars (Table 16.3).

Overall, the highly favourable brand image created by the total advertising and publicity programme contributed towards a highly successful selling performance, well in excess of expectation. Of course, editorial publicity and word of mouth contributed to these high scores; and, of course, the car itself was seen as a good and desirable buy. It is not possible to disentangle the separate effects of advertising, PR and product. But the tone of the advertising set the scene for all the rest.

A volume sales achievement of 16,700 against a target of 12,000 enabled the Metro to obtain 29 per cent of the small-car sector in the launch quarter; and by the end of six months in March 1981, further share growth to 32 per cent made it the highest seller in this sector. Even more importantly, this performance was not obtained at the expense of the Mini, which with 15 per cent during the Metro launch period gave British Leyland an overall 44 per cent of the small-car sector and amply vindicated the decision to keep and target the two models separately. Business results since then continue to justify the dual car strategy. At the end of 1982, despite many competitive new car introductions and improvements, British

Leyland's share of an expanded sector stood at 40 per cent, with the Mini obtaining around 10 per cent.

Conclusions

■ Every successful launch requires a good and innovative product. Every launch is helped by trade and public relations work, by the cooperation of dealers or retailers. But these events do not happen by accident, and they should happen in concert, building on the advertising and each other. A lesson from the Metro launch is that a whole package was put together, and this is what gives a product the best opportunity.

■ Notice also how the initial brief was queried: we can take an independent – and in this case welcome and justified – point of view from that of the manufacturer.

■ The advertising which we developed covered both the emotional (a British car to beat the world) and the rational (this is *why* it is a good buy and so a world-beater).

■ Finally, the concentration of effort at the very first stage of the launch proved correct. Dribbling out the money over six months would never have created the same interest and excitement or have had the same sales effect.

Glossary

ACORN A Classification of Residential Neighbourhoods. This groups small areas into types which depend on the characteristics of the people who live in them. It is based on census data, such as house tenure, social class, age and so on. The analysis is by a firm called CACI.

Adspend The money spent on advertising, usually on media costs only, i.e. excluding the production of the advertisements.

Adstock Roughly, the amount of current and recent advertising for a brand, often in units of thirty-second equivalent TVRs (*q.v.*) per four weeks or per bi-month. The exact definition requires the calculation of the contribution of each previous week's advertising, allowing for a specified rate of decay over the time of its effect (see Half life).

BAR Budget Allocation over Regions: a computer model used by the agency. BAR suggests ways of allocating ITV adspend over the different regions. It allows for different target market values and for different TV costs in the different regions.

Base In modelling (*q.v.*) the response to advertising we fit the observed data by a formula. The constant in this formula is the base. It is the level to which response falls in the absence of causative factors. 'Response' may be sales or a measure in a tracking study (*q.v.*). The fit is approximate and applies for a limited time, so the base may in fact change over time.

BAT Budget Allocation over Time: a computer model used by the agency. BAT shows the effect of a schedule or timing plan on television. It allows for different target market values and for different TV costs at different times of year. It also shows how to improve the plan.

Branding A manufacturer makes a product: a purchaser buys a brand. The difference is the value added by advertising, the pack, history, associations, etc. The product may be changed, by a new formulation for example, but the character or personality of the brand may be the same, or alter more slowly. The task of advertising is often to sustain or enhance or create a brand.

Breakeven The breakeven elasticity (*q.v.*) is determined by the costs of manufacture and other numbers in a brand's budget. If the real elasticity in the marketplace were equal to the breakeven value, then a small change in the relevant decision would make no difference to profit. For example, suppose the breakeven price elasticity were -2. If the real price elasticity, determined by observation of marketplace movements, was also -2, then raising or lowering the price a little may decrease or increase sales volume but does not change profit. If it were -1, then the improvement in volume sales caused by a price drop would not be enough (1 is a smaller number than 2) to compensate the manufacturer for the loss in revenue on each item. If the real price elasticity were -3, then a large enough improvement in volume sales would be produced for the manufacturer to make a greater profit by a price cut.

Buying cycle The typical time between two purchases in a product group by an average purchaser. Thus bread has a shorter buying cycle than holidays. Also used for the processes gone through when deciding to buy.

Client service The department in the agency responsible, among other jobs, for coordinating its work for the client or advertiser. Also called Account Management.

Concept board When the agency has an idea for advertising, be it a positioning for the brand, a mood, a claim, a slogan, etc. it often wants to check it out with the target market. It may also want to clarify the idea internally. A concept board is a sheet of cardboard on which the idea is represented, in words and/or pictures. It differs from a proposition in that the idea gets some of the clothing it will receive in the media. Music or narrative (audio) tapes, reading a script, clips of film, etc. serve similar purposes. Shown in interviews or group discussions, these stimuli help us to predict likely reactions to the finished advertising.

Core group The four people (usually) in the agency who work on a particular brand, and come from these departments: Client Service, Creative, Planning and Media. Others work on the brand too but these are the leaders and represent their departments. Major decisions about the brand involve all members of the core group.

Dip-stick A market research job done to check progress. Often part of a series, e.g. before launch, after four weeks, after twelve weeks; or part of a tracking study (*q.v.*).

Doublehead In making most commercials, the sound (music, voice-overs, effects) is recorded separately from the pictures (an exception is when the characters speak to camera). The picture cut, which is made from the rushes or original shots, is first agreed. Then a doublehead is made, with the sound on one piece of film or tape and the picture on another. Finally a married or answer print is produced.

Elasticity A term used to quantify the relationship between a causative factor (usually price or advertising) and response (usually sales). It is the percentage response change for a one per cent increase in the factor.

It therefore depends on the current level of this factor as well as on the strength of the relationship. If advertising is costing £100,000 a year then a one per cent increase is only £1,000 and may have less effect than one per cent of £1 million. Note that *price* elasticities are almost always negative: a one per cent increase in price causes a loss in sales.

Ex-factory sales Sales of a product are usually measured at two points between manufacture and consumption. Ex-factory is by delivery to a retailer, i.e. leaving the factory or warehouse. Data come from normal accounting procedures. Consumer sales are from the retailer and have to be researched, by audit or survey. Research data from consumers usually fall short of ex-factory data (because of exports and failure to cover all outlets or consumers) and there are pipeline effects causing differences over time.

Generic positioning Often many products can all make very similar claims: they all belong to the same product group. Sometimes a brand wil make one of these claims pre-emptively: it is not really at a great advantage over other products in this respect, but it stakes out an area in its positioning (*q.v.*) and advertising which other brands would be seen as imitative or followers if they repeated.

Half life   In modelling advertising's effects over time, we distinguish long-term (years) from short-term (weeks, months). For the short-term we need a description of how long we are talking about in any particular case. These effects start as relatively large (e.g. in the week after the ad appeared) and then diminish. The half life (measured in weeks) is the time by which half the total, cumulative effect has been felt. An analogy is radioactive decay.

ILR   Independent Local Radio (*c.f.* ITV: Independent Television). The forty or fifty stations regulated by the Independent Broadcasting Authority. Examples: Capital Radio, Severn Sound (for Gloucester and Cheltenham).

Modelling   Representing the real world (example: sales of a brand) by some abstraction. Example: sales share per cent = base + (price elasticity × relative price). There are many different models of varying complexity. They need to be fitted or matched to marketplace data. A model is useful only if it is an accurate representation; this requires it to predict well.

Numerical modelling   The sort of modelling (*q.v.*) where numbers are used; e.g. sales shares, relative price. It is opposed to conceptual models or frameworks which help thinking and discussion, but in which specific numbers − or even definitions − are not used. An example of the latter (now outmoded) is AIDA: advertising works by getting Attention, arousing Interest, creating Desire and leading to Action.

Penetration   The percentage or proportion (of a defined group, usually our target market) who take some defined action. Examples: housewives who have bought our brand since launch; children aged 4−15 who bought in the last six months.

PPI   Personal Purchases Index: a diary panel sold by Audits of Great Britain Limited. This record of sales concentrates on individual rather than household purchases. The data is collected weekly but normally reported by bi-months.

Price sensitivity   A brand's sensitivity (*q.v.*) to its price. This is often its relative price (*q.v.*).

Product innovation   Changing (and presumably improving) the contents or performance of a product. By implication, the change is newsworthy, leads to a competitive advantage and is often part of a product re-launch.

Regression   A statistical technique which examines how one measurement or variable varies with one or more others (for example, how sales share relates to relative price). In *linear* regression, the relationship is a straight line. The fit of the regression is measured by the correlation coefficient: zero if there is no relation, one if the two move exactly together. Even a high correlation does not prove causality. The most common flaw is collinearity. This is when two possibly causative variables move together (*they* are correlated). Only one is the real cause but the second appears to be (especially if the first is omitted in the analysis).

Regional bias   'Regions' are often the ITV or Nielsen areas into which the country is divided. When we study a variable (our sales share, or a competitor's TVRs) we may find it is not equal or evenly distributed over the regions. It is then biased: high in some regions, low in others.

Relative price 'The price' of our brand to the consumer is an abstraction: inflation, different retailers and discounts as well as different pack sizes create a range of actual prices. We usually average our price: so many pounds sterling at the retail level for so many tonnes sold give us our average price per tonne. We can do the same for the whole market, i.e. all similar products, or for a principal competitor whose price is the norm. Our price as a percentage of this standard is our relative price.

Seasonality Variation by time of year. Thus a seasonal market is one with more sales than average at special times, e.g. pre-Christmas. Prices may also vary by season, especially for media.

Segmentation Dividing up (a market, or a group of people). This may be by description (e.g. North v. South), or by action. For example, different manufacturers may decide to change or to emphasize different aspect of their products. If this leads to different types of people buying different products, then they have segmented the market.

Sensitivity This describes the same phenomenon as elasticity (*q.v.*) and is often a synonym, but is not as precisely or numerically defined. A large elasticity means high sensitivity, e.g. to price changes.

TVR Television rating. The percentage of people who are exposed to, or 'see', a commercial when it is transmitted is the rating of that transmission. TVRs vary somewhat by the definition of the 'people' in the target, i.e. we have adult TVRs, housewife TVRs, etc. 'see' is more properly an opportunity to see: some people rated may not actually be present or have briefly switched away from the relevant channel. Adding the TVRs for each spot used gives us the TVRs for a burst or campaign. Thus ten spots averaging a rating of fifteen each give 150 TVRs. Sometimes the length of spots is weighted, so that a campaign of a mixture of ten-second and forty-second spots is reported as producing so many thirty-second-equivalent TVRs.

Tracking study Research among consumers or users carried out continuously (example: 100 interviews every week). Often the main measures are brand and advertising awareness, brand image and usage. These studies enable us to see the dynamics of market movements as well as, by cumulation, providing large samples for usage and attitude data.

Index

Entries in **bold** are defined in the Glossary.